Towering above printers of his time and their
successors for many years afte
figure of Robert Estienne, the

‑xteenth century, whose

‑nd its disse

Robert Estienne's Influence on Lexicography

ROBERT ESTIENNE'S INFLUENCE ON LEXICOGRAPHY

By DeWitt T. Starnes

UNIVERSITY OF TEXAS PRESS, AUSTIN

Published with the assistance of a grant
from the Ford Foundation
under its program for the support of publications
in the humanities and social sciences

Library of Congress Catalog Card No. 63–16061
Printed in the United States of America
by the University of Texas Printing Division
Bound by Universal Bookbindery, Inc., San Antonio

PREFACE

Of the Interchangeable Course, or Variety of Things in the Whole World, and the Concurrence of Armes and Learning, through the first and famousest Nations: from the beginning of Civility, and Memory of Man, to this Present; moreover, whether it be true or no that there can be nothing sayd, which hath not bin said heretofore.

So run the first lines on the title page of a book published in London in 1594. It is characteristic of the period in suggesting the contents of the book and the principle of unity in variety.

But fashions have changed in presenting books to the public, and descriptions of subject matter and puffs for the author which would have appeared on the title page of an Elizabethan publication have been shifted to the preface and the dust jacket. As the title of this book seems to be inadequate and as the expository or descriptive title page can no longer be employed, I resort to a preface to achieve the effect of a Renaissance title page and also to assert that in this book on Robert Estienne there is unity in variety.

My aim is to present evidence to show that Robert Estienne, as an industrious lexicographer, and as an editor of the Bible with indexes and concordances, had a far-reaching influence on lexicographers in England and on the compilers of concordances to the English Bible. The scope of this study does not allow consideration of other countries. Each chapter has, I hope, a bearing on Estienne's two parallel roles—editor and indexer of the Latin Bible and compiler of Latin and Latin-French dictionaries—or on the impact of such work on English lexicographers and other authors. In this diversity of subject matter there is a unity of purpose and thought.

Biographical and bibliographical details, essential to an understanding of Estienne's labors as editor of the Bible and lexicographer general, are presented in Chapter I. Pertinent and significant to this study is the relationship of Estienne's Bible glossary of proper names and his index to the polyglot Bibles of the Renaissance, as described in Chapter II. The Concordance of the Geneva Bible, derived from Estienne, and Minsheu's debt to it, is the subject of Chapter III. Chapter IV shows Cruden's *Concordance* as the consummation of a tradition exemplified in Estienne's early glossary and index and his *Concordantiae* of 1555. Peter Oliver's *Scripture Lexicon* of 1784 reflects the impact of Estienne's *Hebraea . . . nomina* of 1537 and of the Geneva Concordance derived therefrom, as shown in Chapter V. The sixth chapter deals with a special phase of Estienne's work in developing the Latin proper-name dictionary, and the seventh and final chapter endeavors to trace the impact of Estienne on lexicography in England during the sixteenth and seventeenth centuries.

DeWitt T. Starnes

Austin, Texas

ACKNOWLEDGMENTS

For persistent search, beyond the call of duty, for books and journals in our own library and for securing books and photostats from other libraries, I wish to express my gratitude to Miss Kathleen Blow, Chief Reference Librarian, The University of Texas.

I am greatly indebted to Professor James Sledd of Northwestern University for consulting books and making transcripts in the private collection of Mr. Elsdon C. Smith of Evanston, Illinois, and also for sending me information concerning certain books in the Harvard University libraries and for ordering reproductions from some of these. My thanks also to Mr. Smith for a cordial welcome to his collection.

For permission to consult various books, I am grateful to Brown University Library, Harvard University Library, and the Boston Public Library. To Mrs. Ann Bowden and her assistants in the Humanities Research Center, The University of Texas, I am indebted for their courtesy in securing and holding for me books necessary to this study.

To Dr. Lucetta Teagarden, The University of Texas, for a critical reading of the manuscript, for final typing, and for indexing, I am deeply grateful. Without her assistance, this book would be much less free of errors.

D. T. S.

Austin, Texas

CONTENTS

ILLUSTRATIONS

Robert Estienne's Influence on Lexicography

❧ I ❧

The Times and the Man

T HE SPAN of Robert Estienne's life, from 1503 to 1559, comprehended in a remarkable manner the historical events which shaped his career: the Renaissance, the Reformation, and the invention of printing by movable types. His keen interest in the revival of ancient literatures and languages and his training in the art of printing pointed the road he would travel, and the climate of opinion in the Reformation determined his destiny.

Introduction

In its broader aspects the Renaissance had its beginning in the studies of Petrarch and Boccaccio at the end of the fourteenth century.[1] It was marked by a fervent interest in the search for and study and interpretation of manuscripts and books of the ancient Latin and Greek languages and literatures. It was carried on by a host of scholars, native and foreign: by Coluccio Salutati, Sannazaro, and Politian, by Constantine and Janus Lascaris, by Guarino, Vittorino Filelfo, and Marcus Musurus. In the second half of the fifteenth century it was furthered by the founding of the Academies of Florence, Naples, and Rome. In the

---

[1] It is obvious that I am following (with reservations) the traditional view of the Renaissance as set forth by Jacob Burckhardt in *The Civilization of the Renaissance in Italy* and Jules Michelet in *La Renaissance.* John Edwin Sandys gives a slightly different emphasis in *A History of Classical Scholarship,* II. Later discussions of special interest are Erwin Panofsky's "The Renaissance and Renascences," *The Kenyon Review,* VI (1944), 201–236; W. K. Ferguson's *The Renaissance in Historical Thought*; and Henry Harnik's "Three Interpretations of the French Renaissance," *Studies in the Renaissance,* VII (1960).

same period the establishment of the printing press made possible the preservation of precious manuscripts and the more rapid dissemination of classical learning.

One of the best known of the later Italian humanists was Aldus Manutius (1450–1515).[2] Carefully trained in the classical languages at Rome and Ferrara, Manutius early became interested in the master-pieces of newly discovered Greek literature and in manuscripts brought to Italy by Greek refugees from Constantinople. In 1490 he established the Greek press at Venice. With Greek types supplied by Marcus Musurus, the Cretan, and with the aid of Cretan compositors he began printing Greek classics.[3] Within a few years of the turn of the fifteenth century, Manutius published Musaeus, Theocritus, Hesiod, Pindar, Aristophanes, Sophocles, Euripides, Herodotus, Thucydides, Aristotle, and Plato.[4] In 1500 he founded the "New Academy of Hellenists" to promote the study of Greek and the publication of Greek masterpieces. In twenty-one years he produced no less than twenty-seven *editiones principes* of Greek authors and Greek reference works.[5] He died in 1515, but his printing establishment was successfully carried on by his family almost to the end of the sixteenth century. "After little more than a century of beneficent labour in the cause of classical literature, the great house of printers came to an end when the younger Aldus [Aldus Manutius II] died in Rome without issue in 1597."[6] In almost the same period, or from 1502, the printing press of the scholarly Es-tienne family flourished in France and was destined to continue for a much longer period and to achieve perhaps greater renown.

"Even as Petrarch marks the transition from the Middle Ages to the Revival of Learning," writes John Edwin Sandys, "so, in the early his-tory of learning, Erasmus marks the transition from Italy to the north-ern nations of Europe."[7] His life and influence were more closely con-nected with England, France, Italy, Germany, and Switzerland than with his native land. In all of these countries he visited men of learn-ing, and by precept and example evinced his enthusiasm for the new learning or the revival of the study of the ancient languages and litera-

---

[2] Douglas C. McMurtrie, *The Book,* pp. 204 ff.
[3] John Edwin Sandys, *History of Classical Scholarship,* II, 98 ff.
[4] *Ibid.*   [5] *Ibid.,* p. 100.
[6] *Ibid.,* p. 101.   [7] *Ibid.,* p. 132.

tures. He was thus a sort of linking figure, connecting the learning of Italy with that of neighboring countries. He learned much Latin and less Greek, though he never underrated the importance of Greek literature and Greek civilization. He edited Seneca, Suetonius, parts of Cicero, Pliny, and Terence among the Latin authors, Aristotle and Ptolemy in the Greek; he made recensions of St. Ambrose, St. Augustine, St. Chrysostom, and St. Jerome, and an edition of the Greek New Testament. He was a friend of Aldus Manutius in Italy, of Budaeus and the Estiennes in France, of Colet and Linacre and More in England, and of many other humanists. He exemplified the spirit of the Renaissance and he sought to make classical learning and the Scriptures available to all.

The beginning of the Renaissance in England, in the fifteenth century, was marked by travel and study abroad, especially in Italy, and by the collecting of manuscripts and books and depositing of them in England. Among the early exponents of the movement were Humphrey Duke of Gloucester, John Tiptoft Earl of Worcester, William Selling, Thomas Linacre, William Grocyn, William Latimer, John Colet, and Sir Thomas More. Erasmus himself, on a visit to England in 1499, paid tribute to classical authors in England thus:

I have found in England . . . so much learning and culture, and that of no common kind, but recondite, exact, and ancient, Latin and Greek, that I now hardly want to go to Italy except to see it. When I listen to my friend Colet, I can fancy I am listening to Plato himself. Who can fail to admire Grocyn, with all his encyclopaedic erudition? Can anything be more acute, more profound, more refined, than the judgment of Linacre? Has nature ever molded anything gentler, pleasanter, or happier than the mind of Thomas More?[8]

To Erasmus, these scholars exemplified the spirit of the Renaissance in England at the beginning of the sixteenth century. There was in England, however, no scholar or group of scholars editing and interpreting classical texts, and of course no press devoted to printing Latin and Greek books, which could be done more cheaply abroad. An attitude prompted by studies in Italy led Grocyn to discover the spuriousness of the pseudo-Dionysian writings and led Colet to discard the con-

---

[8] Frederic Seebohm, *The Oxford Reformers,* pp. 69–70; cf. Sandys, II, 229.

ventional methods of interpreting the Scriptures and explain Paul's Epistle to the Romans as a human document written for a special audience at a particular period of history.[9] It was an historical and rational approach, as was Colet's interpretation of the Mosaic account of creation by the gospel of accommodation. The rationalistic attitude toward the Scriptures was to find expression in the commentary and notes of Erasmus in his edition of the New Testament (1516). With the coming of the Reformation this liberal point of view became obscured. But "Sixteenth-century English scholars were few, and their steps were halting. Nearly all their inspiration came from the energetic humanism of France."[10]

In France, perhaps more than elsewhere, the introduction of printing promoted the Revival of Letters. As early as 1470 three Germans set up a printing press in the precincts of the Sorbonne. From 1471 to 1472 they printed the works of Florus, Terence, Vergil's *Eclogues* and *Georgics,* Juvenal, Persius, Cicero, and Valerius Maximus. In 1507 Gourmont established a Greek press in Paris and began to publish Greek classics, such as Homer, Hesiod, Musaeus, and Theocritus.[11]

Sir Sidney Lee commented:

At the end of the fifteenth century there was inaugurated that golden age of pure scholarship which is identified with the names of Budaeus, the Scaligers, and the Estiennes. . . . A dozen others deserve mention in the same breath. Greek professorships were founded not in Paris alone, but in numerous provincial universities. Greek manuscripts were collected for Francis I's royal library.[12]

Although almost all the great classical authors were printed for the first time in Italy, France vastly improved on the Italian type of classical scholarship. It is with the scholar-printer family of the Estiennes that we are chiefly concerned. But here we may remind ourselves of the atmosphere in which they labored.

Religious fermentation marked the end of the fifteenth and the first half of the sixteenth century. Heterodoxy was becoming widespread in high and low stations of life. Pomponatius denied the doctrine of the

[9] *Ibid.,* pp. 19–20.
[10] Sir Sidney Lee, *The French Renaissance in England,* p. 18.
[11] Sandys, *History of Classical Scholarship,* II, 167, 170.
[12] Lee, *French Renaissance in England,* p. 18.

immortality of the soul. Scholars trained in classical learning and criticism dared to apply new-found methods to the interpretation of the Bible and the investigation of its history, and to wish for a more correct text than the Vulgate as determined by St. Jerome and believed, among the orthodox, to be correct and infallible. The Inquisition was re-established in Spain in 1483 to ferret out nonbelievers; a convocation was called by the King of England in 1512 to extirpate heresy among the people, but Colet boldly told the assembled clergy to begin the work of reform by amending their own worldly lives. Luther nailed his theses on the Church door and was excommunicated. Calvin established his religious autocracy in Geneva. Orthodox churchmen and theologians saw their world changing into something new and strange. They were alarmed and they used stern measures, even burning at the stake, to halt the change. In such a climate of opinion, Robert Estienne began one phase of his work in the publication of his Latin *Biblia* in 1528.

The Estienne Family

In a significant way the life of Robert Estienne was bound up with that of his family—his father, his brothers, his children, and descendants—for in these, as in himself, was developed and carried on the Renaissance interest in ancient literatures and languages and the printing of correct and beautiful books. The printing establishments which made the name of Estienne celebrated had their beginning in Paris in the first years of the sixteenth century and sustained their reputation with honor in Paris as well as in Geneva until 1664, the year of the last publication of Antoine Estienne.[13] Thus for 162 years, or almost six generations, there was an uninterrupted continuation of remarkable printed works, and the renown of the family persisted even when the later printers of the house of Estienne were not superior to any other good neighborhood printer. Such were the power and repute rightfully acquired by the beautiful, scholarly impressions of Robert and Henri that they brought prestige even to their last descendants, just as the Manutius editions of the late sixteenth century derived their chief credit

---

[13] Antoine Augustin Renouard, *Annales de l'Imprimerie des Estienne ou Histoire de la Famille des Estienne et de ses Éditions* (2d ed.), II, 273 ff.

from the distinctive publications for more than 60 years of the senior Aldus Manutius, his son Paulus, and his grandson Aldus II.

Perhaps the most graphic representation of the Estienne family is found in Antoine Augustin Renouard's briefly annotated "Généalogie de la Famille des Estienne."[14] In this table the name of Henri I heads the list. He is followed by his sons, François, Robert, and Charles. Of these, only Robert had a line of male descendants, including his sons Henri II, Robert II, and François II, through whom the line continued to the end of the seventeenth century.

Henri I, born in Paris about 1470, probably learned the art of printing under the direction of Wolfgang Hopyl, with whom he collaborated in the publication of 3 volumes in 1502 and 1503, and printed, during his career, 121 volumes. He died in 1520, leaving his three sons, François, Robert, and Charles, all of whom had received excellent training in the classical languages, had learned the profession of their father, and had distinguished themselves in varying degrees. Of François very little is known, not even the date of his birth, or whether he was married. Between 1537 and 1548 he was a bookseller and printer, and published some 40 books.[15] François died without heir.

Charles Estienne (?1504–1564) is of more importance to this study because of his relation to his elder and more famous brother Robert (1503–1559) and his family. When Robert was forced to flee to Geneva in 1550 Charles took over the Estienne printing establishment in Paris, with subsequent confusion resulting in the ascription of authorship of some of the books he saw through the press from 1551 to 1561. This topic will be considered in Chapter VI. Charles, like his brothers, had a thorough classical training. He studied medicine and became a *docteur-regent* to the faculty of medicine of the University of Paris, where he was famous for his learning and attracted many pupils. He was an author, or a compiler, as well as a printer, usually gathering his materials from ancient authors and compiling books on medicine, agriculture, and pedagogy.[16] Among his better-known books are *De Dissectione partium Corporis humani* . . . (1550) and *Praedium*

---

[14] *Ibid.,* II, facing 522.   [15] *Ibid.,* I, 97–101.
[16] McMurtrie, *The Book,* pp. 331–332; Renouard, *Annales,* I, 102 ff., II, 253 ff.; cf. William Parr Greswell, *A View of the Early Parisian Greek Press,* II, 204 ff.

Rusticum . . . Lutetiae (1554). The *Praedium* was translated into French by Charles and his son-in-law, Jean Liebault, with the title *L'Agriculture et Maison Rustique*. Charles suffered business reverses and in 1561 became bankrupt. He died, it is said, in 1564 in prison, where he was incarcerated either because of his religion or for debt.[17]

Before our discussion of Robert Estienne, the elder brother of Charles, the immediate ancestor of all the Estienne printers and scholars in the sixteenth and seventeenth centuries, and the central figure in our study, it seems desirable to mention the most renowned member of this celebrated family—Henri Estienne II, the eldest son of Robert. Renouard writes that one of the principal glories of Robert is surely to have been the father of Henri, to have so ably directed his education, and by his noble example to have prepared a way of life so constantly industrious.[18] As a printer, Henri surpassed his father. In his early years he travelled in Italy (1547–1549), and visited Florence, Brabant, and England. A second visit to Italy led to the discovery of ten new books by Diodorus, published in 1559, the year in which Henri succeeded to his father's business in Geneva. Sandys points out that Henri's editions of ancient authors amounted to no less than fifty-eight in Latin and seventy-four in Greek, eighteen of the latter being *editiones principes*. He ruined himself financially, according to Sandys, over the publication of the *Thesaurus linguae* (1572) and the Plato (1578).[19] The *Thesaurus,* in five folio volumes, was his greatest work, the sale of which was damaged by his disloyal assistant, Joannes Scapula, who published an abridgment in one volume.

Though the name of Robert Estienne may be less celebrated than that of his son Henri II, Robert's influence may well have been greater at home and abroad. He had a sound training in the Latin, Greek, and Hebrew languages and a successful apprenticeship in printing under the guidance of Simon de Colines, his stepfather. He had a broad interest in education and religion and sought to promote classical learning by printing the works of good authors and also by compiling dictionaries and grammars to promote knowledge of the ancient literatures. These were adopted by most of the universities of Europe, and

[17] McMurtrie, *The Book,* pp. 331–332; Renouard, *Annales,* II, 361.
[18] Renouard, *Annales,* II, 364.
[19] Sandys, *History of Classical Scholarship,* II, 175.

were also pirated.[20] Robert's ability as a scholar was equalled by his success as typographer. Many of his books were printed with types designed by Claude Garamond and with border initials and ornaments engraved by Geoffroy Tory, all extremely beautiful. He strove for accuracy, however, more than for beauty.[21] In printing the *Biblia* in Latin, Greek, and Hebrew, Estienne's methods and motivations were not unlike those he used in editing Latin and Greek texts of the classics. His was an historical and critical method like that of such humanist scholars as Colet and Erasmus. His motivation was that of the scholar, not the reformer, but his scholarly procedure in printing the Bible led him into difficulties and hardships.

It is important to emphasize the work of Robert Estienne as a printer of classical literature and a promoter of classical learning. This has been well done by a number of scholars: Renouard, Sandys, Douglas C. McMurtrie, and Elizabeth Armstrong. Perhaps less attention has been given to his work as lexicographer and to the lexical aspects of his *Biblia*. A chronological listing of some of his publications in the two fields of Biblical glossing and lexicography indicates the close relationship. Compare the items and dates in the table below:

Date	*Bibles*	*Dictionaries*
1528	*Biblia.* Fol. 2 vols. With glossary of proper names and index of the Old Testament entitled "Hebraea, Chaldaea, Graeca et Latina nomina."	
1530, 1535		*Dictionarium poeticum quod vulgo inscribatur Elucidarius Carminum.*
1531		*Dictionarium, seu linguae Latinae Thesaurus.* Fol.
1532	*Biblia.* Fol. Glossary enlarged. Index of Old *and* New Testaments.	
1534	*Biblia.* Octavo. Copies, with corrections, the 1532 edition.	

[20] McMurtrie, *The Book,* pp. 330–331.
[21] *Ibid.*; Sandys, *History of Classical Scholarship,* II, 173; Elizabeth Armstrong, *Robert Estienne: Royal Printer, passim*; Renouard, *Annales,* II, 287.

Date	Bibles	Dictionaries
1536		*Dictionarium . . . Thesaurus.* Fol. 2 vols.
1537	*Hebraea, Chaldaea, Graeca et Latina nomina.* A glossary of proper names in the Bible and an index of the Scriptures, originally published with the 1528 and 1532 editions of his *Biblia,* now as a separate work, in octavo.	
1538		*Dictionarium Latino-Gallicum.* Fol.
1539, 1549		*Dictionnaire françois-latin.*
1540	*Biblia.* Large fol., fine edition. Contains glossary and index.	
1541		*Dictionarium propriorum nominum.*
1542, 1550		*Dictionariolum puerorum.*
1543		*Dictionarium . . . Thesaurus.* Fol. 3 vols.
1545	*Biblia.* Octavo. 2 vols. With many marginal notes. Glossary and index are much reduced.	*Elucidarius poeticus, siue Dictionarium nominum propriorum.*
1546	*Biblia.* Fol. According to Renouard, a reprint of the 1540 edition.	*Dictionarium Latino-Gallicum.*
1552		*Idem.* Paris, by Charles Estienne, Royal Printer.
1553		*Dictionarium historicum ac poeticum.* Generally ascribed to Charles Estienne but compiled by Robert, as discussed in Chapter VI.

To simplify the illustrations we have omitted from the table a few items such as editions of Estienne's New Testament in Greek and his *Biblia Hebraica* (4 vols., 1534–1544), etc. Only the several editions of his Latin *Biblia,* accompanied with glossaries and indexes, are listed under theological works. Study of the dates in the publications recorded above shows how Estienne's interest in compiling dictionaries and in

Hebræa, Chaldæa,

GRAECA ET LATINA NOMI-
na virorum, mulierum, populorum, idolorum, vrbium, fluuiorum, montium, cæte-
rorúmque locorum quæ in Bibliis leguntur, reftituta, cum Latina interpretatione.

Locorum defcriptio ex Cofmographis.

Index præterea rerum & fententiarum quæ
in iifdem Bibliis continentur.

PARISIIS
Ex officina Roberti Stephani.
M. D. XXXVII.

Fig. 1. Title page from Robert Estienne's *Hebraea, Chaldaea, Graeca et Latina nomina* (1537).

editing the *Biblia* with the proper-name glosses ran parallel during the thirties and forties and how the close relationship was emphasized by the separate publication in 1537 of the Bible glossary, augmented, and with the index of the Old and New Testaments, under the title *Hebraea, Chaldaea, Graeca et Latina nomina.* The history and considerable influence of this Bible glossary, or dictionary of proper names in the Scriptures, is described in Chapter II.

As the Bible glossary, or *Hebraea . . . nomina,* grew out of, indeed was a part of, Estienne's work in editing the *Biblia,* it is pertinent here to give attention to his editions of the *Biblia.* As early as 1523, when he was nineteen years old, Robert served as editor, under his stepfather, Simon de Colines, of the New Testament in Latin. Even then he aroused the ire of the Sorbonne doctors, who termed him an erratic youth and a corrupter of the Scriptures. These attacks continued and intensified with Estienne's successive editions of the *Biblia,* in 1528, 1532, 1534, 1540, 1545, etc., until he was forced to leave France.

Whatever the specious charges and criticisms of the theologians, we may believe that Robert Estienne, in the spirit of the Renaissance scholar-printer, was honestly attempting to make a correct text of the Bible and to make the Scriptures available to more readers. His work was motivated like that of Erasmus' edition of the New Testament (1516) and may well have been inspired by Erasmus' example. In the preliminary matter to his text Erasmus wrote:

. . . other philosophies, by the very difficulty of their precepts, are removed out of the range of most minds. No age, no sex, no condition of life is excluded from this. The sun itself is not more common and open to all than the teaching of Christ. For I utterly dissent from those who are unwilling that the sacred Scriptures should be read by the unlearned translated into their vulgar tongue, as though Christ had taught such subtleties that they can scarcely be understood even by a few theologians, or as though the strength of the Christian religion consisted of men's ignorance of it. The mysteries of kings it may be safer to conceal, but Christ wished his mysteries to be published as openly as possible. I wish that even the weakest woman should read the Gospel—should read the epistles of Paul. And I wish that these were translated into all languages, so that they might be read and understood, not only by Scots and Irishmen, but also by Turks and Saracens. To make them understood is surely the first step. It may be that they might be ridiculed by many, but some would take them to heart. I long that the husbandman should sing portions of them to himself as he follows the plough, that the weaver should hum them to the tune of his shuttle, that the traveller should beguile with their stories the tedium of his journey.[22]

In this period the sentiment expressed by Erasmus and shared by Robert Estienne was heretical. One needs only to recall the climate of religious opinion at the end of the fifteenth and in the early sixteenth century to understand why, by continuous work on the Sacred Scriptures, Estienne became a "controversial" figure. During Estienne's lifetime the University of Paris was steadily declining in both numbers and learning. The faculty of the Sorbonne was gradually being filled by doctors who attempted to conceal their ignorance by striving to attain a reputation of orthodoxy. Some of them denounced the Greek and Roman classics as pagan and strictly maintained that "a knowledge of the Greek and Hebrew languages would operate to the destruction of all religion."[23] Estienne sought to restore the Biblical text by the critical method and made free "use of the emendations and notes of humanist scholars," especially those of Erasmus. The doctors of the Sorbonne thundered against him in their pulpits, but when called upon to point out specific errors in Estienne's editions were seldom able to prove anything but their own inability to translate Greek.[24]

The attacks on Robert Estienne by the Sorbonne divines began with his 1523 Latin New Testament. For his freedom with corrections and his attempts to disseminate the Scriptures, he was suspected of heresy. Each new edition of the *Biblia* or any part of the Scriptures, as the Decalogue, for example, brought renewed attacks and harassment, as Renouard and William Parr Greswell point out. Robert himself wrote that when he published the Decalogue, about 1540, the "orthodox censors" instituted the most rigorous proceedings against him, causing his house to be searched for heretical works and often compelling him to be absent from home, either through apprehension of being arrested or through the necessity of following the king's court and council from place to place in order to counteract the censors' violent designs.[25]

[22] The paraphrase is by Seebohm in *The Oxford Reformers*, p. 203.
[23] McMurtrie, *The Book*, p. 331.
[24] *Ibid.*
[25] Greswell, *A View of the Early Parisian Greek Press*, I, 209.

Renouard holds that Estienne was "persecuted,"[26] not really for the alleged errors in certain passages or for the heterodoxy in the notes and comments, but for his continuous printing of the Scriptures and thus opening to all the entire book of the sacred texts. "C'était là le véritable grief, le motif mal dissimulé des clameurs théologiques; et plus d'un Sorboniste en cela fidèle aux doctrines ultramontaines, trouvait que, pour une telle témérité, le feu n'était pas un châtiment trop sévère."

For years, protected by his own renown and especially by the royal favor, Robert was able to endure. With the death of Francis I, uncertain of the protection of King Henri II, he took refuge in Geneva in 1550, where he found escape from the threat of the heinous theologians.

Estienne's work as lexicographer paralleled that of his Scriptural editing in the 1530's and 1540's. Of the dictionaries he compiled and published in these two decades, first in order of time was the Bible glossary of 1528, later enlarged and published separately as *Hebraea, Chaldaea, Graeca et Latina nomina.*

[26] Renouard, *Annales,* I, 36.

❧ II ❧

Robert Estienne's Glossary of Biblical Proper Names and the Polyglot Bibles

N 1537 Robert Estienne published in octavo the *Hebraea, Chaldaea, Graeca et Latina nomina,* containing (1) a glossary of the proper names—Hebrew, Chaldean, Greek, and Latin —in the Bible and (2) an index to the Old and New Testaments. This book evolved from the author's glossary and index to his Bible (*Biblia,* 1527–1528). The 1537 volume and its interesting history will be discussed later, but as it is closely related to the *Biblia* and its antecedents we must first consider these earlier books.

The Complutensian Polyglot

One antecedent was the Complutensian Polyglot Bible. This work was first published (1514–1517) at Alcala (formerly Complutum) in Spain. Hence the "Complutensian" Bible. The title of the first edition as recorded by Jacques Charles Brunet follows:

Biblia Polyglotta, hebraice, chald., gr., et latin, nunc primus impressa de mandato et sumpt. Fr. Ximeniii de Cisneros curis Demetrii Cretensis, Antonii Nebrissensis . . . In Complutensi universitate, industria Arnaldi Guilielmi de Brocario, 1514–17, 6 vols. in fol.[1]

In a brief analysis of the contents of each volume, Brunet lists, in Volume VI, the glossary of Hebrew, Chaldean, Greek, and Latin words. This glossary is of special interest in our study because it is the basis of the glossary which Estienne supplied for the first edition of his

[1] Jacques Charles Brunet, *Manuel du Libraire et de L'Amateur de Livres,* I, 241.

Biblia (1527–1528). Mrs. Armstrong writes that while preparing this edition of his Bible, "Estienne had at his disposal the Complutensian Polyglot Bible."[2] In his address to the Christian Reader at the beginning of the 1537 independent edition of his glossary, Estienne states clearly his dependence on this Bible. He writes:

Deinde, interpretationem, quae in Bibliis Cōpluti impressis erat, in omnibus fere secuti sumus.

Estienne's clear-cut statement should set at rest the question as to the major source of his glossary; he is, in fact, more than generous. A comparison of the glossary of the 1528 *Biblia* with that in the Polyglot shows a close relationship, but it shows also that Estienne added much to the Complutensian original. When we place side by side the first page of the glossary in the Complutensian Bible and that of Estienne's *Biblia* (1528),[3] we can see at once the similarities of printing patterns and of content: the word lists and explications are printed in Latin, double columns, with the Hebrew and Greek equivalent terms printed in the outer margins. The headings of the word lists, though not identical in phrasing, are much the same:

Complutensian Polyglot (1514–1517): Incipiunt interpretationes hebrai-corum; chaldeorum: grecorumque nominum: veteris ac novi testamenti
. . .

Biblia (1528): Hebraea, Chaldaea, Graeca, et Latina nomina . . . cum interpretatione latina . . .

The Complutensian employs a capital *D* at the end of an entry to denote that the meaning of a word is doubtful, and a *G* to indicate Greek derivation. The editors assumed that the meanings of these symbols would be obvious. Estienne's *Biblia* employs the same letters for symbols but explains the application and meaning.

The Hebrew and Greek marginal word lists correspond closely when glossing the same terms. Estienne's Latin word list in the text proper is based on that in the Complutensian text, though Estienne omits some words of the original, expands some entries, and sometimes supplies

---

[2] Armstrong, *Robert Estienne,* pp. 74, 136–137.

[3] For the comparison of texts I have used photostats from Volume VI of the Complutensian Polyglot (1517) and Estienne's *Biblia* of 1528 in the Harvard University Library.

words not in the original. To be more specific, of the first twenty-six entries in the glossaries of the two texts, twenty-three correspond in choice of Biblical proper names and in explications, though Estienne often expands and makes important additions, which are discussed below. To take another illustration, in the Alcala text between the terms *Aaron* and *Abisag* there are sixty-two entries; between the same terms in Estienne's Bible gloss there are fifty entries. In other words, there are a few terms in each text not to be found in the other, but Estienne frequently gives fuller explications or descriptive details.

Perhaps the most significant innovation which Estienne makes in his Alcala-based glossary is to supply, in abbreviated form, references to the passages in the Scriptures in which the words are employed. The Biblical references thus supplied by Estienne render his glossary more useful to scholars and to general readers of the Bible.

A few parallel entries from the glossaries of the two texts (omitting marginal Hebrew terms) will illustrate the relationship:

Complutensian Bible (1517)

Aaron. Mōs siue mōtanus: aut docēs siue cōcipiens.

Aaronite. Idem. plur. nur.

Aasbai. Confidens in me: vel frater circundans: aut ex hebraeo & Syro frater senectutis.

Aastari. Cursor, . . .

Abba. Pater Syrum est.

Abachuc. Luctator . . .

Abadon. Exterminans, vel perditio.

Abana. Lapideus: vel edificatio: siue pater obsecro nūc.

Estienne Bible (1528)

Aaron, Mons siue montanus: docens, siue concipiens. Filius Amram, exod.6.c.1, para.6.a.

Aaronitae, Idem. pluralis numeri.

Aasbai, Cōfidens in me, vel frater circundans: aut ex Hebraeo & Syro, frater senectutis. Filius Machati, 2 reg.23.d. Heb. Ahasbai, per in secūda.

Abba, Pater, Syrū est. Marc. 14.d. rom.8.c. gal.4.a.

Abadon, Exterminans, vel perditio. Apoc.9.c.

Abana, Lapideus, vel aedificatio siue pater obsecro nunc. Nomen fluuij Damasci, 4.reg.5.d.

Abundant evidence indicates that in making his glossary for the 1528 edition of his *Biblia* Estienne followed the word list—Hebrew, Greek, and Latin—the arrangement on the page, and the general pattern of the Complutensian Bible but that he expanded the original by extending explications and, especially, by citing the specific references to the use of terms in the Scriptures.

In addition to the rather extensive glossary for the 1528 *Biblia,* Estienne supplied indexes. The title page reads: "Indices item duo, alter in Vetus Testamentum, alter in Novum." And the general heading runs "Index rerum et sententiarum, quae in Veteri Testamento continentur." Estienne seems to have compiled several Scriptural indexes or little concordances—one each for the Old Testament and the New Testament and one for the Epistles and the Gospels. I know of no source for these except the Bible and Estienne's own glossary. By 1532, when he published the second edition of the *Biblia,* he had combined the Old and New Testament indexes into one, as a sentence on the title page explains: "Index copiosissimus rerum et sententiarum vtriusque Testamenti." This new index is so changed in wording and so expanded that it is difficult to see the relationship to the 1528 text, and the author continued to modify and change the Biblical index in later editions.

The heading for the glossary in Estienne's 1532 folio edition of the *Biblia,* beginning, "Hebraea, Chaldaea, Graeca et Latina nomina,"[4] copies verbatim part of the heading from 1528, slightly expanding the original. The glossary proper, with the word list and explications in Latin and the Hebrew and Greek equivalents in the outer margins, follows the pattern of the earlier edition of the *Biblia* and of the Complutensian Polyglot.

The 1532 glossary corrects, expands, and adds entries to that of 1528. *Abarim,* for example, is expanded from 3 lines to 10½; *Abel* is expanded 1 line; *Abel-main,* 2 lines; *Abel-mehula,* 1 line; *Abel-sittim* (*Abel-satim*) is added as a new item of 5½ lines; *Achaia* is expanded 4 lines; *Achaz,* 1 line; but *Achzib, Achazib* is corrected and reduced 4 lines. These augmentations are typical; the process of correction and augmentation continues throughout the glossary.

---

[4] From a copy of the 1532 *Biblia* in the British Museum.

The *Biblia* of 1534, in octavo, with double columns—intended to be a portable format—is a reprint of the 1532 folio text. Though there are some useful corrections, the small size of the pages necessitated suppression of part of the marginal notes and of the glossary of Hebrew, Greek, and Latin words.[5]

The fine folio edition of the *Biblia* of 1540 has some further corrections, but the text of the glossary is essentially that of 1532. The heading has the language verbatim of the *Hebraea . . . nomina* (1537), which was a slight modification of the 1532 text.

Estienne published a Vulgate edition of the Bible in 1545 (2 vols., octavo), *"Biblia* sacra latina: juxta veterem & vulgatam editionem."[6] Although the text is accompanied by elaborate marginal notes containing variant readings and erudite commentaries, the glossary and the index of subjects are very brief. Under the heading "Hebraicorum, Chaldaeicorum, Graecorumque nomine interpretatione" is the Hebrew word list, giving succinctly in Latin the primary meanings, without references to specific passages of the Scriptures. Similarly, the much reduced index shows little relation to the earlier indexes or glosses of the *Biblia,* or to the separate publication of glossary and index in the octavo volume of 1537.

Since this 1537 volume is central to this phase of our study it is necessary to give a detailed description of it. Here is the wording of the title page:

Hebraea, Chaldaea, Graeca et Latina nomina virorum, mulierum, populorum, idolorum, vrbium, fluuiorum, montium, caeterorumque locorum quae in Bibliis leguntur, restituta, cum Latina interpretatione. Locorum descriptio cosmographis. Index praeterea rerum & sententiarum, quae in iisdem Bibliis continentur. . . . Parisiis Ex officina Roberti Stephani. M. D. XXXVII.[7]

On a leaf (Sig. Aij) following the title page is this heading: "R. Stephanus Christiano Lectori. S." Estienne here explains to the Chris-

---

[5] Renouard, *Annales,* I, 39–40.

[6] I have used a copy of this edition in the Humanities Research Center, The University of Texas.

[7] For this study, I have used my own copy of the *Hebraea . . . nomina* (1537). Only four other copies, so far as I can discover, are found in American libraries. These are in the Newberry, the University of Illinois, the Harvard University, and the Union Theological Libraries.

O
T

עתי Othei, Tempus vel hora mea, aut iniquitas mea. Filius Ammiud filii Amri,1.para.9.a

עתר Othir, Excellens,fiue refiduus,aut remanens. Nomé viri,1.para.15.b

עתני Othni, Tempus fiue hora mea.Nomé viri,1.par.26.a

עתליהו Otholia, Tempus domino, fiue hora domino. Filiu Icroam,1.para.8.c

עתניאל Othoniel, Tempus dei, fiue hora dei. Filius Cenez fratter Caleb,iof.15,d.1.para.4.c

Z

עזה Oza, Fortitudo, aut capra. Horti nomen,4.regu.11.d. Nomen viri,1.paral.6.a.8.a

עזא Oza,Idem.Filius Abinadab,2.reg.6.a

עזן Ozan,Fortitudo earum, aut capra earum. Pater Phaltiel principis tribus Iffachar,num.34.d

עזזיהו Ozaziu,Fortitudo domini. Nomen viri,1.paralip.15.c.17.c

אזן שארה Ozen-fara, Auricula carnis vel cõfanguinitatis,aut auricula fermentata vel remanés, fiue flaéra carni vel confanguinitatis aut refidui. Vrbscondita à Sara filii Ephraim,1.para.7.c

עזי Ozi, Fortis, vel fortitudo mea, aut hircus meus. Filius Bocci filii Abifue,1.para.6.a.Filius item Thola filii Iffachar,1.para.7.a.vide & 9.b

Ozi,1.cõd.3.f,Tunc,fiue aut ifte.Nomen viri.

עזיה Ozia, Fortitudo domini fiue hircus domini.Filius Amafie regis Iuda,3.reg.26.a:qui 4.reg.15.a,dicitur Azarias.Filius Caath filii Leui,1.para.6.b

עזיאל Oziel, Fortitudo domini.Nomen viri,1.par.6.b

עזיאל Oziel, Fortitudo dei, fiue hircus dei. Filius Bela filii Beniamin filii Iacob,1.paral.7.b. Filius Caath filii Leui,exod.6.c.Vide & 1.para.4.g.1.para.23.c

Oziel,Idem.num.3.d.1.para.26.c

עזיאלי Ozielita,Idem.num.3.d.1.para.26.c

אזני Ozni, Auris vel aufcultatio mea, fiue flaéra. Filius

---

c.3 filii Iacob,num.26.b

Oznieza, Idem.num.26.b

Oziel,1.para.17.c,Adiutoriũ dei,fiue atriũ dei. Patet Ierimoth.

עתניאל

P

Paphos, Bulliens,vel æftuans, G. Nomen infulæ, πάφος
Palæfthina,Confperfa,fcilicet cinere vel puluerefiue ruina appofita,vel ruina duplex,aut ruinæ potus, vel cécidit bibens. Eft ea Syriæ regio, quæ Hebraice dicitur Philifthiim,ad mare mediterraneum pertingens, fita ad occidétem Iudææ. Author eft Iofephus lib.1.Iudaicarum antiq.cap.11. de hac Pomponius Mela in 1.Plinius in 5.cap.12.& 13.

פלשת Palæfthini, Idem. p.n.m.g.genef.11.d, Populi quos Interpretes nonnunquam Philifthæos,nonnunquã ἀλλοφίλους,id eft alienigenas, vocant.

Palmyra, Hebraice dicitur Thamor, & interpretatur palma, vel dacaylus, aut commutatio vel permutatio, fiue amaritudo. Vrbs Syriæ nobilis, quæ & Hebraice aliæ Thadmor dicitur.

תדמר Palmyra, Hebraice, Thadmor, interpretatur confeffio vellaus amaritudinis, aut confeffionis vel laudis myrrhæ:fiue ex Hebræo & Syro, laus præceptoris vel domini.fiue ciuitatis in Syria, quam ædificauit Salomõ, 1.reg.9.c.1.para.8.a:quæ aliàs Thamor fiue Thafmar dicitur Hebraice.Hæc ab Hadriano principe,Hadrianopolis dica fuit.

Pamphilia, Tota dilecta vel amabilis. G.Prouincia Afiæ ab ortu Ciliciam habet, ab occafu Lyciam & Afiæ minoris partem, à feptentrione Galatiam & Cappadociam,à meridie mediterraneũ, quod illic Pamphilii mati nomen habet.Tota Tauri expatiatis iugis fepta.De hæc Ptolemæus lib.5.Plinius lib.5.cap.17.Pompo. Mela o.iii.

Fig. 2. An opening from Robert Estienne's *Hebraea, Chaldaea, Graeca et Latina nomina* (1537), showing Hebrew and Greek words in the margins.

INTERPRETATIO.

Zethu, Oliuetum. Nomen viri, 1.ef.d.10.a
Zethua, Idem. Nomen viri, 1.ef.d.1.a

Z
I

Zit, Sudor, aut tremor. Nomen viri, 1.para.5, b
Zina, Fornicatio: aut Syriace, nutriméntum vel armá. Nomen viri, 1.para.1.3. b

Zio, Ifte:vel Syriace, fplendor, aut claritas. Nomen fecundi menfis, qui Aprilis apud nos dicitur, 3.reg.6.a

Ziph, Iftud os, vel ifta bucca: aut Syriace, falfitas, vel falfus. Duæ funt huius nominis in tribu Iuda ciuita. res: ex quibus altera nomé magnæ dedit folitudini, Iof. 15; d. & g.1.reg.23; b: quam ædificauit Roboam,1.paral. 2.f.2.para.11.b

Zipha, Idem. Filius Ialeleel,1.para.4.c
Ziphæi, Idem.p.n.1.reg.23;c

Ziza, Vniuerfalis vel omnimodus, feu beftia, vel fera aut refplendés: vel Syriace, recedés. Filius Ionathan filii Iuda filii Onam,1.par.2.e. Eft & nomen principii, 1.para.4.f

O

Zoheleth, Reptans, vel trahens, Rupes eft iuxta fontem Rogel nomine, 3.reg.1.b

Zoheth, Separatio, aut ifte ftupens vel pauidus, feu ifte confraëtus:vel ex Hebræo & Syro, ifte defcendén. Filius Iefi,1.para.4.d

Zonzommin, Scelus vel turpitudiné cogitátes, feu fcelus fceleratorum. Populi funt qui aliàs ab Ammoni. tis Raphaim nuncupantur, deut.2.d

Zoom, Abominás, vel immundus. Filius Roboam ex Abihail,1.para.11.d

Zorobabel, Alienus à côfufione, aut aliena vel extranea confufio, fiue extranea cômiftio, aut difperfio con fufionis vel commiftionis, feu circulus commiftionis vel confufionis. Dux in Iuda,agg.1.a.Filius Phadaia fi lii Iechoniæ,1.para.3.c.1.ef.d.2.a

V

Zuzim, Poftes, vel fupetliminaria, aut fplendétes: vel

Syriace, recedentes, aut pecuniæ. In gen.14. non eft no men proprium.1. x x enim, gentes fortes: Chaldæus in terpres, robuftos interpretatur. quod & annotauit Hie ronymus in quæftionibus in Genefin, dicens fic debe re legi in eo loco, Et robufti in Ham. vt fit proprium lo cinon autem legatur In eis.

R. Stephanus Lectori S.

Indices duos aliquando compofueramus Chariffime lector:alterum in Vetus,alterum in Nouum teftamentum: quorum priorem quòd non omni ex parte abfolu tus effet, deintegro collegimus, & eundem Noui tefta menti indici permifcuimus, fingula in fua loca diftribuentes: ne tibi moleftum effet nunc Veteris nunc No ui de eadem re indicem confulere. Ea autem indicis col ligendi canfa fuit, vt ex collatione locorum vtriufque teftamenti ob oculos pofitorum, facilius poffis genuinâ eorum quæ optes, nancifci intelligentiam. Nam præter literarum ordiné in fingulis dictionibus obferuatum, communes locos ita fere digeffimus, vt magnum ex ip fo ordine ad facrarum literarû cognitionem adiumen tum tibi acceffurû putemus. Boni igitur côfule quicquid eft laboris, & Vale.

INDEX RERVM ET SENTENTIARVM
Veteris & Noui teftamenti.

A & adfunt, apoc.1.b.17.
Aaron, enos, & eius filii. exod.28.b
Aaronis filii Nadab & Abiu accidunt, quod ignem a-
lienum offerunt. leuit.10.a
Aaron quem ipfi adorant. exod.32.a
Aaron obiurgat Moyfen ob vindicatam cæ
dem Moyfæ cum deo loquentem. exod.16.b
Aaron iuftus ab Ifraelitis conftituitur. exod.16.g

Aaron & Eliorum mortis exp-
ctant Moyfen cum deo loquentem.
exod.16.b
Aaron & Eliorum dies ornatus.exod.
18.1.a
Aaron iuftus ab Ifraelitis conftituitur.exod.
Aaronem,quem ipfi adorant.exod.32.a
Aaron obiurgat Moyfen ob vindicatam cæ
dem.exod.16.b
Aaron iuffu dei, it obuiam Moyfi prof.
ducit in Ægyptum.exod.4.g

FIG. 3. An opening from Robert Estienne's *Hebraea, Chaldaea, Graeca et Latina nomina* (1537), showing the end of the proper-names glossary, the second address to the reader, and the beginning of the index to the Old and New Testaments.

tian Reader that he will find the Hebrew proper names revised and corrected by the Hebrew codices and made consistent with the names in the Scriptures themselves. In almost all of these he has followed the Complutensian Bible. As in the earlier edition, a doubtful interpretation is followed by the letter *D*, a word of Greek origin by the letter *G*. In the description of places he has followed the best ancient authorities, such as Ptolemy, Pliny, Pomponius Mela, Strabo, Josephus, and Volaterranus, and more recent authorities, such as Jacobus Ziglerus, Wolffgang Weissembergius, and Andrea Althamerus. Estienne concludes: "Fruere igitur Lector, & vale" ("May the reader use and enjoy this book! Goodbye").

The text proper, which follows this address, has the running title "Interpretatio—Nom. Heb. Chal. Graec. et Lat." The text follows the pattern of the glossary in the 1532 *Biblia,* except that the octavo is printed in single columns on the page, with the word list and explications or descriptions in Latin and the Hebrew and Greek equivalents in the outer margins. Specific Biblical references to both Old and New Testaments are carefully cited to show where words are used, and there are also citations of classical and medieval authorities when descriptions go beyond the Scriptural texts.

The second part of the 1537 *Hebraea . . . nomina* contains the index of the Bible. It has this heading: "Index Rerum et Sententiarum Veteris & Novi testamenti." This text is also preceded by an address to the reader in which Estienne explains that he had formerly made two indexes, one for the Old and another for the New Testament.[8] The index for the Old not being adequate, he had made it anew ("de integro") and had here joined it with the index of the New in one alphabetical arrangement so that the reader would not have the labor of consulting first one index and then the other.

This index, in much smaller type than the glossary in the first part of the volume, is printed in double columns on the page and is more elaborate and probably more useful than any other index Estienne had printed with the *Biblia* thus far.

What were the sources of the 1537 glossary and index? The title of the book, given above, suggests its origin. This volume grew out of

[8] Estienne had in fact already combined the two indexes in the 1532 *Biblia.*

the glossaries and indexes that were made for editions of the *Biblia* published before 1537. In this connection Mrs. Armstrong writes: "The original *interpretatio* printed with his Latin Bibles (together with the indexes) was collected in 1537 into a stout octavo volume, Hebraea, Chaldaea, Graeca et Latina nomina virorum . . . qui in Bibliis leguntur."[9] This general statement is correct, but we can be more specific: the glossary and index printed with the 1532 *Biblia* were the actual sources of the matter in the separate and independent book of 1537.

The 1537 index makes some rearrangements to adjust to the new octavo format and to expedite consultation. It also expands some of the 1532 entries and adds others. Specific references to the Bible are kept and sometimes augmented, but, throughout, the 1532 text is basic. Of more importance to this study, the 1537 text follows closely that of 1532, which, as shown, was an expansion of 1528. In the 1532 glossary of the *Biblia* there are sixty-six entries between the letters *Aa* and *Ac;* in the 1537 volume are the same number of entries, corresponding in content and Biblical references as well as in the marginal Hebrew and occasional Greek equivalents. There are, however, some slight adjustments in the word list. The earlier glossary, for example, sometimes has two spellings for a single entry, as in *Abel-mehola, Abel-mehula; Eben-bohan, Aben-boën.* In each instance, the 1537 text enters only the second term of these, as *Abel-mehula.* Similar results appear in a comparison of the fifty-four entries in each of the texts from *Amaad* to *Amram.* In short, all tests show that the glossary and index of the 1537 volume are based upon similar materials in the 1532 *Biblia.* We shall now trace the persistence of the 1537 glossary in the polyglot Bibles and the Geneva Bible of the sixteenth and seventeenth centuries.

The Antwerp Polyglot

On the verso of the title page in my copy of Estienne's 1537 *Hebraea . . . nomina* is a pencilled note by a former owner or bookseller which reads, "Taken from the apparatus of the Antwerp Polyglott." This note was provocative and puzzling to me. I found that a polyglot Bible (8 vols., folio) had been published by the Plantin Press, at Ant-

[9] Armstrong, *Robert Estienne,* p. 90.

werp (1569–1572).[10] The anonymous note would have Estienne borrowing from a work published ten years after his death. It is true that his Bible glossary of 1528 followed the pattern and used most of the content of the glossary in the 1514–1517 Alcala, or Complutensian, Polyglot and expanded it, but the *Biblia* of 1532 continued the process of augmenting individual entries and adding new ones until much of the glossary was new matter added by Robert Estienne. It was this glossary which, with very slight changes and with the index, was printed independently in 1537. And this glossary the editors of the Antwerp Polyglot followed closely. They thus took what Estienne had borrowed from the Alcala version, plus what he had added, and the writer of the anonymous note had the cart before the horse. The Antwerp Polyglot of 1572 took its glossary and part of the preliminary matter from Estienne's 1537 volume; Estienne did not take from the Antwerp.

The title page previously quoted from the *Hebraea . . . nomina* (1537) may be compared in phrasing and content with the following heading for the Antwerp glossary (1572):

Hebraea, Chaldaea, Graeca et Latina Nomina Virorum, Mulierum, Popvlorum, idolorum vrbium, fluuiorum, montium, caeterorumque locorum quae in Bibliis vtriusque Testamenti leguntur in veteri interprete . . . Locorum praeterea descriptio ex Cosmographis.

Except for part of a sentence omitted above, this heading follows verbatim the wording of Estienne's 1537 title page. Furthermore, the Antwerp editors take over, with modifications, Estienne's address to the Christian Reader. Compare these headings:

Estienne: R. Stephanus Christiano lectori. S.
Antwerp: Typographus Christiano lectori. S.

Antwerp substitutes "Typographus" for "R. Stephanus" and thus conceals the original author's name. Although Antwerp elaborates on

[10] The first part of the title obviously has the same wording as that of the Complutensian Polyglot of 1517, beginning "Biblia Polyglotta, hebraice, chald., gr. et lat. . . ." The item in Brunet's bibliography which follows his analysis of the Complutensian Bible is listed thus: "Eadem, hebraice, chald. gr. et lat.; cura et studio Benedicti Ariae Montani. Antwerp., Plantin, 1569–72. 8 vol. infol." This refers to the Antwerp Polyglot, which, though patterned on the Alcala, contains eight volumes instead of six, and differs in other respects, e.g., as to glossary.

the context of Estienne's original address, it copies part of the advice to the reader, word for word. Compare the following passages:

Hebraea . . . nomina (1537)	*Antwerp Polyglot* (1572)
Ad haec omnia accessit locorum diligens descriptio ex optimis quibusque authoribus, Ptolemaeo, Plinio, Pomponio Mela, Strabone, Josepho, Volaterrano: & recentioribus . . . viris in hac re diligentiss[imis].	. . . in quo praeter diligentem locorum descriptionem ex optimis quibusque auctoribus, Ptolemaeo, Plinio, Pomponio Mela, Strabone, Josepho, Volaterrano, & quibusdam recentioribus viris in hac re diligentissimis.

Here the borrowing by Antwerp is obvious. Even more pertinent is the fact that the Antwerp editors follow the pattern—originally of the Alcala text—used by Estienne of placing the Hebrew and Greek terms in the outer margins and using the Latin for entries and explications. Worthy of more emphasis is the fact that the Antwerp text follows the 1537 *Hebraea . . . nomina* of Estienne in the word list and Scriptural citations. The expanded description of *Abarim* (1537) reappears in the Antwerp, as does the new entry *Abel-satim*. The procedure is similar throughout: in making their glossary of the 1572 Antwerp Polyglot Bible, the editors have preferred what they found in the *Hebraea . . . nomina* (1537) to the earlier Estienne Bible glossary of 1528 or to any other antecedent.

An index printed in Volume VII of the Antwerp Polyglot has the general title "Index Biblicus," and was apparently compiled by Ioannes Harlemius, who gives instructions to the reader on how to use the index. Though this has much in common with the Estienne index, which Harlemius may have consulted, there is no evidence of a close and consistent following of Estienne's index.

It is sufficient here to emphasize that the glossary of Hebrew, Chaldean, Greek, and Latin words in the Antwerp Polyglot is based directly upon Estienne's *Hebraea . . . nomina*. In the account which follows, we shall trace further the fortunes of this 1537 octavo volume.

The London Polyglot

About seventy-five years after the publication of the Antwerp Polyglot Bible a somewhat similar work was printed in London under the editorship of Brian Walton. For convenience in distinguishing among the polyglot Bibles in this discussion I have adopted, without precedent so far as I know, the title the "London Polyglot." The wording of the title page reads as follows:

Biblia sacra polyglotta, complectentia. Textus originales, hebraicum, cum pentateucho samaritano, chaldaicum, graecum. Versionumque antiquarum, samaritanae, graecae . . . chaldaicae, arabicae, aethiopicae, persicae, vulg. lat. Quicquid comparari poterat. Cum textuum & versionum orientalium translationibus latinis. Ex vetustissimis mss. undique conquisitis . . . Cum apparatu, appendicibus tabulis, variis lectionibus, annotationibus . . . Opus totum in sex tomos tributum. Edidit Brianus Waltonus, S. T. D. . . . Londini, Imprimebat Thomas Roycroft, 1657. 6 vols., folio.[11]

In the Preface (*Praefatio*) Walton surveys the work of his predecessors in editing the Bible, paying tribute to the work of Robert Stephanus (Estienne) for his Greek New Testament, to Münster, and to others. He mentions with respect the Complutensian Polyglot, but he shows greater esteem for the Antwerp Polyglot. He writes: "Palmam omnium eruditorum consensus tum his tum reliquiis praeripiunt Antwerpensis Regia . . . 1571." It is significant that, for Walton, the Antwerp edition takes the palm from all others.

Publication of this work was finished in 1657, and the editor was granted a charter of exemption from taxation on publishing his Polyglot for a period of five years. According to Brunet,[12] Walton referred to Cromwell in a passage of the Preface, immediately before the list of persons who had encouraged the work. After the Restoration certain changes were made in the preliminary matter, and the name of Charles II replaced that of Cromwell. As copies containing the reference to the Protector are rare, we here quote the Latin of the original Preface:

Primo autem commemorandi, quorum favore chartam a vectigalibus immunem habuimus, quod quinque ab hinc annis, a concilio secretiori primo concessum, postea a Serenissimo D. Protectore ejusque concilio, operis promouendi causa, benigne confirmatum et continuatum erat . . .

---

[11] I used the fine copy of the "London Polyglot," edited by Brian Walton, in the Humanities Research Center, The University of Texas.

[12] Brunet, *Manuel du Libraire,* I, 342.

The text within the engraving reads:

S.S
BIBLIA
Polyglotta
Complectentia Textus Originales

HEBRAICOS cum
Pentat. Samarit:
CHALDAICOS
GRÆCOS.

Versionumq Antiquarum.

SAMARIT.   GRÆC. SEPT.
CHALDAIC.   SYRIACÆ.
LAT. VULG.   ARABICÆ.
ÆTHIOPIC.   PERSICÆ.

Quicquid comparari poterat.

Ex
SS Antiquis undiq Conquisitis opti
misque Exemplaribus impressis summa
fide collatis.
Edidit
Brianus Waltonus S.T.D.
Anno M.DC.LVII.

FIG. 4. Engraved title page from Brian Walton's polyglot Bible ("London Polyglot," 1657).

After the Restoration this statement was suppressed and the following substituted:

Inter nos effusiore bonitate labores nostros prosecuti sunt (praeter eos quorum favore chartam a vectigalibus immunem habuimus) . . . Serenissimus princeps D. Carolus [etc.]

Now the name of Prince Charles heads a list of patrons who made possible the completion and publication of the great Polyglot, and in this revised list the name of Oliver Cromwell does not appear. Other names, to mention a few, are William Count Hereford, Baron Beauchamp; Master William Lenthall, Keeper of the Rolls; John Selden of the Inner Temple, London; George Count of Rutland; Mildmay Count of Westmoreland; and Thomas Lord Fairfax, Baron de Cameron.

After the list of benefactors, Walton continued with these words:

To God, the father of light, from whom comes every good and perfect gift, we offer most devout thanks that he has granted us health and strength to bring to completion this sacred work, a monument of Religion and Letters, [and, paraphrasing Horace, he concludes:] a monument more durable than brass and higher than the royal Pyramids, which neither eroding shower, nor northern wintry blast, nor the innumerable succession of years and the flight of time can ever destroy.

In the above discussion of the Antwerp text we noted that the editors adapted, for the heading of their Bible glossary, the title page of Estienne's 1537 *Hebraea . . . nomina,* also adapted and elaborated his address to the Christian Reader, and followed his word lists and descriptions, making only slight changes. If we place side by side the first pages of the glossaries in Walton's London Polyglot and in the Antwerp, we shall see at once that Walton took over verbatim the heading, the address to the reader as it had been modified from Estienne, and also the word lists and descriptions. Although Walton, as his *Praefatio* shows, knew well Estienne's editions of the Bible and doubtless the glosses and vocabularies, he preferred to follow the Antwerp text. His ultimate debt is nonetheless to Robert Estienne's *Hebraea . . . nomina,* or 1537 glossary of the Bible.

To illustrate more specifically the relationship, we may note that the headings of the glossaries in the Antwerp and the London texts begin:

"Hebraea, Chaldaea, Graeca et Latina nomina" and conclude with "Locorum praeterea descriptio ex Cosmographis." The phrasing between is also identical. Following the general heading, this subheading, which is the same in each text, is centered:

Typographus Christiano lectori. S.

There follows in each text the address proper, beginning: "Ne quid tibi esset, Christiane lector," and ending with "Feliciter vtere hoc libello, ac vale." Again, the phrasing throughout is identical. And both the heading and the address to the Christian Reader are adaptations of what first appeared in Estienne's *Hebraea . . . nomina.* Again, a comparison of the first six entries—*Aaron, Aaronitae, Asbai, Abadon, Abana, Abarim*—in Estienne, Antwerp, and London texts gives further evidence of the close relationship. The pattern of printing in double columns, with the Hebrew and Greek terms in the outer margins, is continued, and these terms correspond, except that in Estienne's octavo of 1537 the author has fewer words in the margins.

Although Walton's debt to Estienne in his glossary is indirect via the Antwerp Polyglot, it is interesting to test in another way the correspondences to Estienne's *Hebraea . . . nomina,* that is, by the number of entries under certain letters of the alphabet. Under *F,* for example, there are only 3 entries in each text; under *G,* 158 in Estienne, 159 in Walton; under *L,* 75 in Estienne, 78 in Walton; under *Z,* 65 in Estienne, 64 in Walton. Under other letters, such as *A* or *C* for example, there is a wider gap in the number of entries. But what is important here is that the Estienne Bible glossary was basic to the London glossary, though the Antwerp edition was Walton's immediate source.

The Antwerp edition, however, was not the source of Walton's index of the Scriptures. For this he seems to have turned directly to Estienne—to the index printed with the *Biblia* (1528) or to that published in the 1537 *Hebraea . . . nomina,* or possibly to both. The heading Walton employs indicates his preference for the latter work. Compare these headings:

Walton: Index Rerum et Sententiarum Veteris ac Novi Testamenti.
Estienne: Index Rerum et Sententiarum Veteris & Novi Testamenti.

A comparison of the two indexes from which these headings are transcribed will show that (1) the Estienne 1537 index is much more elaborate than Walton's; (2) there are, notwithstanding, hundreds of close correspondences of words and phrases and of references to Scriptural passages; (3) Walton employs Arabic numerals to indicate chapter and verse, whereas Estienne follows an earlier tradition of using a numeral and a letter, as *"Abba, pater . . .* rom.8.c. gal.4.a." (Walton: *"Abba, pater . . .* rom.8.15. galath.4.6.")

Walton's tendency to condense what he found in the Estienne index is apparent from the beginning. He follows closely Estienne's first brief entry, *"A & [Omega]* deus"; then *Aaron,* for which Estienne has 22 separate entries, each with specific references to the Scriptures, Walton reduces to a single comprehensive entry: *"Aaronis* acta leguntur, exod. 4.14.28 & 29.4.32.," etc., these references deriving, apparently, from those cited after the various short entries in Estienne. The third entry in the London Polyglot index is *"Abalienari* a Deo. Isa.1.4. Osea.9.10.," which duplicates Estienne's first entry after the *Aaron* entries. Of Estienne's 2 entries on *Abdemelech,* Walton chooses one and follows it closely.

Walton's method of using Estienne as a basic source for his index, as illustrated under the letter *A,* is observable throughout the other letters of the alphabet—condensation of several short entries on a given topic to a single entry with the appropriate references, selection of one entry from two or more, condensation of a long entry to a shorter one, correction of specific references. Noteworthy is the reduction of the number of entries under the letter *G.* Here Estienne has more than 300 entries, Walton only 84. Under *Gaudium,* for example, Estienne has 25 entries and illustrations; Walton chooses 7 of these. Under *Gloria,* Estienne has 65 references in their contexts; of these Walton chooses 11. In Estienne's index, under *Q* are 13 entries, in Walton nine; under *Z,* Estienne has 35, Walton, 26.

Walton borrowed freely from Estienne's index, but he was no slavish follower. He selected or omitted freely, he supplied material of his own, he corrected errors and eliminated verbiage, and thus he produced a very useful Biblical index.

This section of our study has been limited to the relationship of Estienne's Bible glossary and index (*Hebraea . . . nomina,* 1537) to similar apparatus found in the polyglot Bibles of the sixteenth and seventeenth centuries. The possible relationship of his editions of the *Biblia* (1528, etc.) to the texts of the polyglots, rewarding as the subject might be, I have no intention to explore. It is well to recall, however, that Estienne's *Biblia* found its pattern and initial word list in the Complutensian Polyglot, published at Alcala (1514–1517). The glossary of this *Biblia* was expanded and developed and published, independently, with Estienne's Biblical index in 1537. The glossary in the 1537 volume was taken over, with slight changes, by the editors of the Antwerp Polyglot (actually, only another edition of the Complutensian), published by the Plantin Press (1569–1572). The glossary thus adapted was employed by Walton in his London Polyglot of 1657.

In the chapters which follow we shall trace the relationship of Estienne's proper-name glossary and index (*Hebraea . . . nomina*) to the Concordance in the Geneva Bible, to Minsheu's *Guide into Tongues,* and to Cruden's *Concordance.*

❦ III ❧

Estienne: Geneva Concordance, Minsheu's *Guide, Scripture Names Expounded*

URING the last years of his life Robert Estienne lived in Geneva and continued his work as printer and publisher. He went to Geneva because he was in sympathy with the religious ideas of John Calvin and his circle. He knew Calvin's *Institutes of the Christian Religion* and other works, and printed some of these in Geneva. Calvin and his friends were familiar with Estienne's editions of the *Biblia,* its commentaries, glossaries, and indexes, and with his dictionaries.

Also at Geneva during the 1550's were a considerable number of Marian exiles—educated men, seeking to escape religious persecution, to maintain religious freedom, and to promote the Christian faith through the dissemination of the Scriptures in their native tongue. They looked for guidance to men like Estienne, formerly Royal Printer in Paris, renowned scholar and editor of the Bible, and Calvin, Biblical commentator, interpreter, and critic. This climate provided inspiration for the English translators, William Whittingham, Anthony Gilby, and Thomas Sampson, whose collaboration produced the famous Geneva Bible.

The Geneva Bible was first published in quarto in 1560. Following the pattern of the original, many editions were printed in quarto; others appeared in folio and in octavo. In its various forms and sizes it became immensely popular, and by 1644, it is estimated, 150 edi-

tions had been printed in England and abroad.[1] Quarto editions printed
after 1578 are of special interest, for in December of this year an important adjunct was supplied and printed as an independent but closely
related supplement to the Geneva Bible, namely, two alphabetical
tables, constituting a concordance. Between 1581 and 1615, *STC* lists
15 editions of the quartos with the term "Concordance" on the title
page of the Bible proper.

The Geneva Concordance

Although in its word lists and numerous Biblical references, the
Concordance was designed to assist readers of the Geneva Bible, it was
not compiled by the original Bible translators and editors. It was printed
by Christopher Barker or his deputies or, later, by his son Robert, mo-
nopolistic printers of Bibles,[2] and always had its independent title page
and the signature of the compiler. The title page begins thus: "Two
right profitable and fruitfull Concordances, or large and ample Tables
Alphabeticall." The author explains that the First Table is concerned
with the proper names, Hebrew, Chaldean, etc., in the Bible, together
with the Scriptural references or "common places." The Second Table
comprehends "all such other principall words and matters as concerne
the sense and meaning of the Scriptures." Together the two tables con-
stitute a concordance near to present-day meaning of this term. On the
title page the author explains that the tables will serve for the "Translation called Geneva" and also for the other translation [*i.e.* Bishops'
Bible] "authorized to be read in Churches." He then refers us for
further information to the "Preface to the Christian Reader," and concludes, "Collected by R. F. H."

In the two-page Preface the author refers to these "two Alphabets

[1] See the informative article by the late Professor E. M. Clark on "Early
Geneva Bibles in the University of Texas Library," *The Texas Quarterly,* II,
(Winter, 1959), 167 ff. Estimates of the number of editions of this Bible vary.
J. R. Dore (*Old Bibles,* 2d ed.) guesses 200 editions; Nicholas Pocock (*Quar-
terly Review,* 178 [1894], 164) suggests 130 editions; T. H. Darlow and H. F.
Moule (*Historical Catalogue,* I, 61) estimate at least 140 editions; Rollins and
Baker *(English Renaissance),* 150 editions.

[2] For an account of the Barker family's monopoly on the printing and sale
of Bibles in England from 1576, see Alfred W. Pollard's *Records of the English Bible: The Documents Relating to the Translation and Publication of the
Bible in English, 1525–1611,* pp. 223–224.

of directions vnto common places hereafter following" which "I haue in maner of a briefe Concordance, collected, digested, and caused to be imprinted for thy commoditie." There follows an exposition of the two tables and their value in assisting the reader to acquire an adequate knowledge of the Scriptures. At length he concludes: "This xxii of December. An. Domini. 1578. Thine in the Lord, Robert F. Herrey." No person of the name "Robert F. Herrey" has been discovered in the second half of the sixteenth century. There is reason to believe that this name is a pseudonym, but we shall refer to Herrey as the author.

After the Preface there begins on the following page (Sig. A^3) the First Table of the Concordance—the proper names—69 pages of 2 columns each; at Sig. E^3 begins the Second Table—an index of common nouns and phrases with references to supporting Scriptural passages—111 pages of 3 columns each. The two tables cover 180 pages containing 471 columns—a sizable concordance, which is the same for most of the Geneva black-letter quarto Bibles after 1578.

What connection has the Concordance prepared by Herrey, as an adjunct to the Geneva Bible, with Robert Estienne's Bible glossary and index published in 1537 under the general title *Hebraea, Chaldaea, Graeca et Latina nomina?* The relationship is definitely suggested by the phrasing of parts of the title page and by the address to the Christian Reader. Herrey's English sentences are paraphrases of Estienne's Latin.

Estienne

Title Page: Hebraea, Chaldaea, Graeca et Latina nomina . . . quae in Bibliis leguntur, restituta cum Latin interpretatione.

Address to the Christian Reader: Hebraica propria nomina restituta, quae in Bibliis vtriusque testamenti sparsa leguntur.

Herrey

Title Page: The first table contayning the interpretation of the Hebrue, Caldean, Greeke, and Latine wordes and names scatteringly dispersed throughout the whole Bible.

Preface to the Christian Reader: . . . all the strange names and wordes to be founde here and there throughout the whole Bible remayning written in the Hebrewe, Chaldean, Syrian, Greeke and Latin Languages.

Herrey's reference to the "names scatteringly dispersed throughout the whole Bible" is fairly close to Estienne's "nomina . . . in Bibliis vtriusque testamenti sparsa leguntur." Herrey's insertion of "Syrian" in the second quotation derives from the context of Estienne, who in his glossary frequently refers to the Syrian origin of a word.

Another illustration of the close relationship of the two authors, or of Herrey's dependence on Estienne's Latin, may be seen in the comparisons which follow.

Estienne writes in his title page, "Hebraea . . . nomina virorum, mulierum, populorum, idolorum, vrbium, fluuiorum, montium, caeterorumque locorum, quae in Bibliis leguntur . . .," and in his address to the Christian Reader he writes, "Praeterea so nomen viri incidit, si foeminae, si populi, aut idoli, si vrbis, prouinciae, regionis, fluuij, denique etiam si montis . . . annotatum est." Herrey, in his Preface to the Christian Reader, says, "[One may find] the name of any Man, Woman, Countrey, Citie, Place, River, Idol, . . . in the same conteyned."

The fact that Herrey shows familiarity in his title page and Preface to the Christian Reader with the corresponding items in Estienne's *Hebraea . . . nomina* is in itself of no great significance, but it is important in suggesting Herrey's close study of the Estienne text rather than that of the Antwerp Polyglot Bible of 1572. The Antwerp borrowed its word list and index very literally from Estienne, but it did not have in it the examples cited here which are common to Estienne and Herrey. As a basis for his Concordance, Herrey used the convenient octavo volume of Estienne's *Hebraea . . . nomina.* From this he translated the Latin literally. He claims no originality; he names no authorities; he has "collected" his materials, he tells us. Although he may have employed more than one source, the bulk of his Concordance derives from Estienne. The illustrations which follow (corresponding Biblical references are omitted) show Herrey translating literally for the First Table of his Concordance from the proper-name glossary of Estienne's *Hebraea . . . nomina.*

(1)

Herrey: *Abarim, goings ouer, furors, or conceiuing*: or in the Syrian
      tongue, *All kinds of corne.* A hill ouer Jordan, where the
      Israelites pitched the 41 mansion in the wilderness.

Estienne: *Abarim,* Transitus, . . . siue transeuntes: aut furores, vel preg-
nantes: aut Syricae, frumenta. Mons est Moabitarum contra
Jericho, supra Jordanem . . . vbi Israelitae castra fixerant XLI
mansione Eremi.

(2)

Herrey: *Abel-Shittim, sorow of thornes,* A place not far from Jordan,
south from the Moabites, so named of the plenty of thornes
growing there.

Estienne: *Abel-satim,* Luctus spinarum, luctus declinationum; aut praevari-
cationum . . . Non procul a Jordane locus in deserto ad me-
ridiem Moabitarum, a spinarum copia habens nomen.

(3)

Herrey: *Iapho, fairenesse, or comelinesse,* The name of both a hauen and
Citie . . . called Ioppa. The Barbarians now call it Sappho.

Estienne: *Ioppe,* Pulchritudo, aut decor. Oppidum in ora curae Syriae in
monte situm, vna cum portu, qui a Barbaris nunc Sappho
appellatur.

(4)

Herrey: *Italie,* A country so called of King Italus, or of Italis, signifieth
with calves, for that it aboundeth with calves.

Estienne: *Italia,* Ab Italo rege dicta est: vel a *Italis,* id est vitulis, eo quod
illa regio vitulis abundet.

(5)

Herrey: *Og,* rosted bread, or a mocke: or after the Syrians, *holding down
or hindered.* A great gyant, king of Bashan.

Estienne: *Og,* Subcineritius panis vel torta, aut subsannatio: vel Syriace de-
tentus aut impeditus. Rex Basan.

(6)

Herrey: Potiphar, In the Aphrican tongue *a bull.* Syrian, Hebrew &
Chaldee, *a fat bull or the fructifying of fatnesse.*

Estienne: *Phutiphar,* Aphricae taurus: aut ex Syro & Hebraeo, saginatus
taurus, vel pinguedinis fructificatio. Eunuchus Pharaonis.

(7)

Herrey: *Tiberias, a good vision, a nauel, or a breaking asunder,* A citie of
Galilee by the sea Tiberias, taking name thereof, Ioh.6.1.,
sometime called (as Ioseph. Antiq. cf.c.18) Genessareth: it
was builded by Herode the Tetrarch in honor of Tiberias
Cesar, and called after his name.

Estienne: *Tiberias*, Bona visio, vel umbilicus, aut confractio. D. Vrbs Gali-
laeae ad mare sita, quod ab sita civitate appellatur mare Ti-
beriadas, iohan. 6. Hanc civitatem olim Cenereth appellatam,
Herodes Tetrarcha in honorem Tiberii Caesaris condidit, teste
Iosepho in 18.Cap.4. antiq. Iudaic.

The examples above show the simpler type of borrowing used in the
First Table, which deals with proper names. Herrey translates directly
from Estienne's Latin glossary for the Hebrew, Chaldean, etc., names,
but the majority of the entries in the First Table contain much matter
not in Estienne's glossary. For the additional details, Herrey uses the
second part of Estienne's volume, that is, the *Index rerum et sententiarum Testamenti veteris et Novi*. In treating such words as *Aaron,
Abraham, Ahab* (*Achab*), Herrey takes matter from both sources in
Estienne and combines these in his First Table. For *Aaron,* for example,
Estienne has in his glossary a statement of the Hebrew primitive
meaning and two lines besides. In the index, however, Estienne has 21
items concerning Aaron and his deeds. Herrey draws matter from both
entries and places all of it under *Aaron* in the First Table. To supple-
ment *Jeroboam* in his First Table, Herrey translates 19 items from the
Estienne index. Perhaps one detailed example will best show how
Herrey paraphrased and combined materials from the two parts of
Estienne's book:

Herrey: *Ahitophel* [*Achitophel in margin*], *brother of ruine, which
lacketh, which is forsaken, or hath need, or a brother without salt, savour, wisedom or grace.* A counsailour of Dauid,
who conspired with Absalom against him. 2 Sam. 15. 12. His
counsaile was counted as an oracle of God. 2 Sam. 16. 13. His
counsaile giuen to Absalom was confounded by Hushais con-
trary counsaile, by which means Absalom perished. 2 Sam. 17.
1, 7, 14. He hanged himself because his counsaile was not
accepted. 2 Sam. 17. 23.

Estienne: *Achitophel*, Frater ruinae, vel frater defectus, aut frater insipidi-
(Gloss)   tatis, id est rei insulsae. Consiliarius regi Dauid. 2 reg. 15. b.
Pater Eliam. 2 regum. 23. d.

Estienne: Achitophel consiliarius Dauid stat a parte Absalom. 1 reg. 15.
(Index)   b. c.

Achitophel consilium, tamquam verbum dei habitum. 2 reg.
16. d.
Achitophel consilium nocte irruendum esse super Dauidem
dum duodecim milibus: deus dissipat per Chusai dantem
aliud quo pererit Absalom cum suis. 2 reg. 17. a, b, c.
Achitophel laqueo se suspendit quod non fuisset factum
consilium suum contra Dauidem. 2 reg. 17. f.

Having completed his First Table (proper names) by translating
and combining materials from both the glossary and index of Estienne,
Herrey could then deal in the Second Table with the common nouns,
including abstract names and topics left in Estienne's index—and there
were thousands. Incidentally, in making his Second Table, he had opportunity for free expansion and, particularly, for introduction of
topics not treated in Estienne's original index, but Estienne was still
the major source. For example, for *Arke* (Second Table), Herrey translated 21 items from Estienne, 5 of which related to Noah's ark and 16
to the Ark of the Covenant.

Of Estienne's 40 items with their Biblical references under *Gloria,*
37 are translated under *Glorie* in the Second Table. *Gratia,* with 23
items in Estienne, is represented by 18 of these under *Grace,* in Herrey.
In such entries as *Predestination, Justification, Reprobation, Reprobate, Elect,* and *Election* a Calvinistic bias is revealed. From evidence
I have gathered, examples of which are presented here, my conclusion,
not heretofore voiced by anyone else, is that Herrey based his Concordance firmly upon the glossary and index in Robert Estienne's
Hebraea . . . nomina of 1537.

Herrey's use of the Estienne items under the entry *Lex* (*Law*) offers
a concrete illustration of his procedure. In the transcription which
follows, Biblical references are omitted.

Lex (*Law*)
(1)
Herrey: Moses repeateth the Law.
Estienne: Legem explanat Moyses.

(2)
Herrey: Moses commanded the Lawe for an inheritance of the congrega-
tion of Iaakob.

Estienne: Legem praecipit Moyses haereditati dei.

(3)

Herrey: Cursed be hee that confirmeth not all the words of the Law, to doe them.

Estienne: In Legis, sermonibus qui non permanserit, nec eos opere perfecerit, maledictus sit.

(4)

Herrey: God commandeth to reade the Lawe day and night and why.

Estienne: Legem suam vt nocte & die legat vt sciat quid gerere debeat, praecipit deus.

(5)

Herrey: We ought alwayes to haue the Lawe before our eyes, and in our hearts.

Estienne: Lex in corde & ob oculos semper habenda.

(6)

Herrey: Moses exhorteth the people to keepe the Law.

Estienne: Ad Legem seruandam adhortatio Moysi.

(7)

Herrey: The Law of the burnt offering.

Estienne: Lex holocausti.

Minsheu's *Guide Into Tongues*

Although John Minsheu may well have known Robert Estienne's Biblical word lists as recorded in the *Hebraea . . . nomina* (1537), his debt to the French lexicographer is indirect, coming by way of Herrey's Concordance, as printed in black-letter quarto editions of the Geneva Bible from about 1580. Near the end of the title page of the *Guide,* Minsheu writes:

Item, There are added the Etymologies of proper names of the Bible, Adam, Eve, Cain, Abel, Seth, etc., with the Etymologies of Countries, Cities, Towns, Hills, Rivers, Flouds, Promontories, Ports, Creekes, Islands, Seas, Men, Women, Gods, Peoples, and other things of note.

Neither in this statement nor elsewhere does the compiler indicate what version of the Scriptures, or index or concordance he used to supply the proper names from the Bible. His language suggests, however, his familiarity with the Concordance ascribed to Robert F. Herrey.

The word lists ascribed to Herrey first appeared in 1578 with the title:

Two right profitable and fruitfull Concordances, or large and ample Tables Alphabeticall. The first conteining the interpretation of the Hebrue, Caldean, Greeke, and Latine wordes and names scatteringly dispersed throughout the whole Bible, with their commonplaces [i.e., book, verse, and line references to the Scriptural passages in which the names appear] following euery of them: the second comprehending all such other principall wordes and matters as concerne the sense and meaning of the Scriptures.

In his Preface to the Christian Reader, Herrey writes, "I haue together placed by themselues . . . all the strange names and words to be found here and there, remayning written in Hebrew, Chaldean, Syrian, Greeke, or Latine languages." A little further on in the Preface Herrey, instructing his reader in the use of the tables, or Concordance, writes, ". . . thou art to resort alphabetically to the first of them, with the name of any Man, Woman, Countrey, Citie, Place, Riuer, Idol, etc., in the same conteyned." This admonition seems to anticipate by almost half a century the language of Minsheu quoted above.

From about 1580 to 1615 the Herrey Concordance was printed, with its independent title page and colophon, in most black-letter quarto editions of the Geneva Bible, to which it was definitely keyed. These editions had on the title page the words: "The Bible . . . with Annotations . . . and also a most profitable Concordance." *STC* lists, between 1605 and 1621, ten editions of the Concordance, which may have been printed independently.

Whether Minsheu or his assistants used an independent Herrey text or that published with the Geneva Bible, the following illustrations will show that the First Table (proper names) in Herrey's Concordance was a principal source for the Bible names in the *Guide* (1627).

(1)

Minsheu: *Abarim* . . . i. transitus. A hill beyond Jordan, where the Israelites pitched the 41 mansion in the wilderness, Num. 33. 47. from whence God shewed Moses the land of Chanaan, Num. 27. 12. and vpon which hill Moses died. Deut. 32. 49, 50 & 34. 1. 5.

Herrey: *Abarim. goings ouer* . . . A hill ouer Jordan, where the Israelites pitched the 41 mansion in the wildernesse. Numb. 33. 47. from whence God shewed Moses the land of Canaan. Num. 27. 12. and vpon the which hill Moses died. Deu. 32. 49, 50 and 34. 1, 5.

(2)

Minsheu: Cesarea or Caesarea, a city so called because built by Caesar, one called Cesarea Stratonis, Acts. 9. 30 & 10.1. 12. 19. & 21. 8. an other named Philippi, Matth. 16. 13. Marke 8. 27. because Philip the Tetrarch built it: an other Cesarea the head citie of Cappadocia, Acts. 8. 22.

Herrey: *Cesarea. a lush of haire.* A citie surnamed Stratonis. Acts 9. 20 & 10. 1. and 21. 8. and 12. 19. Also another surnamed Philippi. Matth. 16. 13, Mar. 8. 27. Because Philip the Tetrarch builded it. Also another Cesarea is the head citie of Cappadocia. Acts 18. 22.

(3)

Minsheu: Daniel, i. the judgment of God (Heb.) He deliuereth Susanna from the two wicked judges, Dan. 13. 45. he destroieth Bel and his temple, and slew the dragon, Dan. 13. 1–28. he is cast into the Lions Denne, Dan. 6. 16 & 14. 29. his accusers are cast in and deuoured, Dan. 6. 28 & 14. 42. the Vision of the foure beasts signifying the foure Monarchies is declared vnto him, Dan. 7. 1, 17.

Herrey: *Daniel. judgement of God.* The sonne of Dauid by Abigail. 1 Chro. 3.1. [Here I omit twelve lines in the column which are not used by Minsheu]. Hee is cast into the Lyons den. Dan. 6. 16 & 14. 42. The vision of the foure beasts signifying the foure Monarchies is declared vnto him. Dan. 7. 1. 17. . . . . Hee deliuereth Susanna from the two wicked Iudges. Dan. 13. 45. He destroieth Bel and his temple, and slew the dragon. Dan. 13, 1–28.

For clearness in presenting the foregoing examples, I have omitted Hebrew, sometimes Greek, words and phrases and kept to the English in the two texts. It is obvious that Minsheu follows closely the language of Herrey's Concordance and employs the same Scriptural references. For *Cesarea*, Minsheu corrects Herrey's reference ("Acts. 9. 20." to "Acts. 9. 30") but makes a mistake of his own in transcribing Herrey's reference of "Acts 18. 22." as "Acts. 8. 22." Under *Daniel,* Minsheu uses only the latter half of Herrey's entry, changing the order of details but retaining the Biblical references. In many instances, Minsheu selects items from Herrey and reduces verbiage, as in *Eleazar, Elias,* and *Elijah.* Sometimes he translates Herrey's English into Latin, keeping the Scriptural references, as in *Damascus, Hosanna, Ieroboam.* Whatever his procedure, his main source is generally Herrey's Concordance. And the Concordance, as we have shown, was based directly on the Biblical word lists in Estienne's *Hebraea . . . nomina* of 1537.

Scripture Names Expounded

Some of Minsheu's readers may have recognized the source of the Biblical names in his *Guide into Tongues.* Minsheu himself makes no mention of his use of Herrey's Concordance. About thirty years after the second edition of the *Guide* (1627) an abridged edition of Herrey's Concordance was published, under the title of *Scripture Names Expounded.* Unfortunately, no copy of this work is now available though we can learn much about it from the transcription of its title page in a modern bookseller's catalogue. In 1960 H. W. Edwards, Bookseller, Ltd., (England) offered for sale a book which bore no date but which he placed *circa* 1660 and which was described thus:[3]

SCRIPTURE NAMES EXPOUNDED, in this right profitable, fruitfull, large and ample Alphabeticall Table: Containing the Interpretation of about foure thousand Proper Names (but halfe a dayes Reading in Newcastle, July 16, 1649) in the Hebrew, Caldean, Greeke, and Latine Tongues, dispersed throughout the whole Bible. Collected by R. F. H. Now again rePrinted by S. D. for the benefit of all that would soone Reade and understand the Scriptures of Truth, in their Originall Tongues, specially Hebrew; these Names contain all, or the most of the Primitives in Hebrew, which being all known, with their Significations, make a firmer impression of them in memory, than in anyway else I know, all Names being reduced to their Primitives, which in a moneth one unlettered in the Hebrew, may doe by a few directions, with much ease, profit, and delight.

---

[3] The copy of *Scripture Names Expounded* offered for sale by Edwards was acquired by Dr. Wilbur N. Smith, Pasadena, California. Dr. Smith reported to me in a letter dated January 31, 1962, that his copy has been misplaced or lost and is therefore not now available to interested persons.

From the foregoing description, it is obvious that *Scripture Names Expounded* is an abbreviated edition of the Concordance or Tables Alphabeticall collected by R. F. H. (i.e., Robert F. Herrey), with only the First Table, of proper names, being included. The Concordance thus revised and "now again re-Printed by S. D." attained some popularity in its day. Who S. D. was, we do not know. His revised edition of Herrey's Concordance is echoed in a book entitled *The Scripture Lexicon,* first published in 1784. But this is to anticipate.

❧ IV ❧

Estienne: Cruden's *Concordance*

LEXANDER CRUDEN was born at Aberdeen in 1701 of Scotch-Presbyterian ancestry.[1] He was educated at an Aberdeen grammar school and Marischal College, from which he received the M.A. degree. In 1720 he showed signs of insanity, from unrequited love, and was kept under restraint for a period. He appeared as a private tutor in London (1722) and later as amanuensis to the Tenth Earl of Derby, by whom he was discharged on account of his ignorance of French. He was a tutor on the Isle of Man, and then bookseller at the Royal Exchange, London, 1732.

In 1737 he published his *Concordance*.[2] Disappointed in the expected patronage of his book, he became temporarily insane and was

[1] See the biographical sketches in *DNB* and in the Preface to *Cruden's Concordance to the Old and New Testaments* (unabridged ed.) published by Fleming H. Revell Company, Westwood, New Jersey, in 1958. This modern edition is a reprint of Cruden's second (1761) edition.

[2] The date usually cited for publication of the first edition of Cruden's *Concordance* is 1737, although the *British Museum Catalogue* lists the date of the earliest edition as 1738 and that of the second edition as 1761. The copy I have used, in the Humanities Research Center, The University of Texas, has on the title page the date MDCCXXXVIII (1738). No other date is given, either on the title page, in the dedication to Queen Caroline, or in the Preface. The 1761 edition has clearly spelled out on the title page: "The Second Edition." If there was an edition printed in 1737 and another in 1738, the 1761 edition would be the third edition. Such information as is available suggests that there was a token printing of the *Concordance* in October or November, 1737, but that the first edition proper was printed early in 1738. Thus the second edition was printed in 1761 and the third—little more than a reprint of the second—in 1769. Cruden died in 1770 and could hardly have been responsible for revisions made after 1761.

A COMPLETE

CONCORDANCE

TO THE

HOLY SCRIPTURES

OF THE

Old and New Teſtament:

IN TWO PARTS.

CONTAINING,

I. The APPELLATIVE or COMMON Words in ſo full and large a manner, that any Verſe may be readily found by looking for any material Word in it. In this Part the various *Significations* of the principal Words are given, by which the plain Meaning of many Paſſages of Scripture is ſhewn: An Account of ſeveral *Jewiſh* Cuſtoms and Ceremonies is alſo added, which may ſerve to illuſtrate many Parts of Scripture. II. The PROPER NAMES in the Scriptures. To this Part is prefixed a TABLE, containing the *Significations* of the Words in the Original Languages from which they are derived.

To which is added,

A CONCORDANCE to the Books called APOCRYPHA.

The Whole digeſted in an eaſy and regular Method; which, together with the various SIGNIFICATIONS and other Improvements now added, renders it more uſeful than any Book of this kind hitherto publiſhed.

The SECOND EDITION, with conſiderable Improvements.

By ALEXANDER CRUDEN, *M. A.*

Search the Scriptures, for in them ye think ye have eternal life, and they are they which teſtify of me. - John v. 39.

Thou haſt known the holy Scriptures, which are able to make thee wiſe unto ſalvation, through faith which is in Chriſt Jeſus. All Scripture is given by inſpiration of God, &c. 2 Tim. iii. 15, 16, 17.

LONDON:

Printed for J. KNAPTON, C. HITCH and L. HAWES, H. WOODFALL, A. CRUDEN, A. MILLAR, J. BUCKLAND, J. WHISTON and Co. J. BEECROFT, J. FULLER, B. DOD, J. HINTON, J. RIVINGTON, W. JOHNSTON, J. RICHARDSON, T. LONGMAN, G. KEITH, J. FULLER, jun. S. CROWDER and Co. B. LAW and Co. T. FIELD, E. DILLY, R. and C. WARE, and J. WREN. MDCCLXI.

FIG. 5. Title page from Alexander Cruden's *Concordance* (1761).

placed in a private asylum in Bethnal Green. After his escape in 1738 he found employment correcting works of learning for the press. Soon he styled himself "Alexander the Corrector" and believed himself divinely inspired to reform the nation. He wrote pamphlets on his experiences and on contemporary events and worked intermittently on the revision of his *Concordance,* a second edition of which he published in 1761 and a third in 1769. In 1770 he was found dead in his lodgings in Camden Passage, Islington, kneeling against a chair, in an attitude of prayer.

To compile a Biblical concordance so elaborate as Cruden's, with so many thousands of Scriptural references and illustrative transcriptions, would be well-nigh impossible for one man in his lifetime. Cruden did not attempt such a task. He did not invent the system of recording the Scriptural references; he did not select the words or topics to be presented, nor the illustrative sentences to be transcribed. These things had been done by his predecessors in the field. His work was to verify and correct, to extend contextual matter, and to rearrange conventional materials. In this procedure, his book may be said to mark the consummation of a tradition of two hundred years—from Robert Estienne in 1537 to Alexander Cruden in 1737.

Although Cruden acknowledges direct indebtedness to no one, his survey of concordances in the Preface of his first edition reveals specific knowledge of his predecessors—of Robert Estienne, of John Marbeck, of Thomas Wilson, of Clement Cotton, of Samuel Newman. He probably knew at least one other authority not mentioned in the Preface— Robert F. Herrey. To what extent did Cruden make use of the works of his antecedents? How far was he indebted, directly and indirectly, to Robert Estienne? What was his own contribution? This study represents the only thorough consideration of the sources of Cruden's *Concordance* which has ever been attempted. If we begin with a concordance near in time and content to Cruden's *Concordance* and work backward to the beginnings of the sixteenth century, noting the relationship of each to its antecedents, and attempting to show the unity of purpose, technique, and content, perhaps some of the answers to the foregoing questions will become clear. Let us begin with what I term the "Cotton-Newman *Concordance*" of 1658.[3]

---

[3] Samuel Newman (1600?–1663), B.A., St. Edmund's Hall, Oxford, 1620;

Little information is available concerning Clement Cotton and his work. In the *Dictionary of National Biography* there is no independent sketch on him, though he is referred to in the *DNB* essay on Samuel Newman, on the title page of Newman's *Concordance,* and in the preliminary matter of the text. William Gouge refers to Cotton's book as "A Complete Concordance of the whole Bible (1631)" with a separate section for the Apocrypha.[4] In 1643 Samuel Newman published, in folio, with his initials, "A Large and Compleat Concordance to the Bible . . . according to the best translations. First collected by Clement Cotton, and now much enlarged . . . 1643." Other editions, with Cotton's name as the first collector on the title page, were published in 1650 (folio), 1658 (folio), and 1683 (quarto). This last edition is often called the "Cambridge *Concordance.*" I refer to the work in all its editions as the "Cotton-Newman *Concordance.*"

Cruden owes much to the Cotton-Newman *Concordance.* "A Large and Compleat Concordance to the Bible in English" becomes in Cruden "A Complete Concordance to the Holy Scripture of the Old and New Testament: in Two Parts." Newman, following Cotton, had arranged his *Concordance* with common and proper names in one alphabet and a concordance of the books of the Apocrypha at the end. Similarly, Cruden places the index of the apocryphal books last in his arrangement.

Unlike Newman, and following an earlier tradition, Cruden presents his materials under two alphabets: (1) the appellatives or common words, and (2) the proper names. The relatively short proper-name section (forty pages) Cruden further divides into two parts: (a) "an alphabetical table containing the signification of the words [proper names] in the original languages from which they are derived," and (b) Scriptural references to sources of the proper names. For the definition-essay sketches and primitive meanings of proper names Cruden goes back to sixteenth-century antecedents, but the part with Scriptural

---

nonconformist minister; emigrated to New England, 1636; in 1644 became the first minister of Rehoboth, Massachusetts, where he died in 1663.

[4] The *Catalogue* of the British Museum lists other editions also, in quarto, of the Cotton *Concordance* printed by the "Assignes of Clement Cotton," in London, in 1633, 1634(?), 1635, and 1638.

references to proper names is simply a rearrangement of matter from the Cotton-Newman source, as is the Apocrypha.

For the bulk of what he calls his "appellatives," or common words, constituting about nine-tenths of his book, Cruden also follows the Cotton-Newman *Concordance.* Unlike his source, however, Cruden often inserts a definition immediately before the Scriptural references, explaining in one-two-three order the various meanings of the word as it is employed in the Bible, or an account of it based on non-Biblical sources, as, for example, in *Fear, Faith, Fall, Kingdom, Lion, Mandrakes, Synagogues, Tabernacle.*

Comparison of the series of entries below will show beyond a doubt the close dependence of Cruden upon the Cotton-Newman text.

(1)

Cruden (1737):

COLT, S.

Gen.	32.	15.	thirty milch camels with their *c*.
	49.	11.	binding his asses *c*. to the choice vine
Judg.	10.	4.	Jair had 30 sons that rode on 30 *c*.
	12.	14.	Abdons sons rode on 70 ass *c*.
Job.	11.	12.	tho' man be born like a wild asses *c*.
Zech.	9.	9.	riding upon a *c. Mat.* 21. 5. *John* 12. 15.
Mat.	21.	2.	ye shall find an ass tied, a *c*. with her, Mark 11. 2. *Luke* 19.30.
		7.	brought the ass and *c*. and set him, *Mar.* 11. 7.
Mark	11.	5.	what do ye loosing the *c. Luke* 19. 33.
Luke	19.	35.	they cast their garments on the *c*.

Cotton-Newman (1658):

COLTS

Gen.	32.	15.	thirty milch camels with their *colts*
	49.	21.	and his asses *colt* to the choice vine
Job	11.	12.	tho. man be born like a wild-asses *colt*
Zech.	9.	9.	riding upon a *colt*, the foale of an asse
Mat.	21.	2.	find an asse tyed with a *colt*, loose them
		5.	sitting upon an ass, and a *colt*, the foal of
		7.	they brought the asse, and the *colt*
Mar.	11.	2.	shall find a *colt* tied whereon never Luke 19. 30
		4.	went their way, and found the *colt* tied

5. what do ye loosing the *colt*, Luke 19. 33
7. they brought the *colt* to Jesus, and cast

Lu. 19. 33. as they were loosing the *colt*, the owners
35. and they cast their garments upon the *colt*

Joh. 12. 15. thy Ki. cometh sitting on an asses *colt*

Asse colts

Jud. 10. 4. had 30 sons, that rode upon 30 asse *colts*
12. 14. Abdons sons rode on seventy asse *colts*

(2)

Cruden (1737):

ENLIGHTEN

Psal. 18. 28. the Lord my God will *e.* my darkness

ENLIGHTENED

1 Sam. 14. 27. and Jonathans eyes were *e.* 29.
Job. 33. 30. to be *e.* with the light of the living
Psal. 97. 4. his lightnings *e.* the world
Isa. 60. 1. arise, be *e.*, for thy light cometh
Eph. 1. 18. eyes of your understanding being *e.*
Heb. 6. 4. impossible for those who were once *e.*

Cotton-Newman (1658):

ENLIGHTEN

Psal. 18. 28. God will *enlighten* my darknesse

ENLIGHTENED

1 Sam. 14. 27. and his eyes were *enlightened*
29. see, mine eyes have been *enlightened*
Job 33. 30. to be *enlightened* with the light
Psal. 9. 74. lightnings *enlightened* the world
Ephes. 1. 18. your understanding being *enlightened*
Heb. 6. 4. those who were once *enlightened*, and have

(3)

Cruden (1737):

ESPOUSALS

Cant. 3. 11. crowned him in the day of his *e.*
Jer. 2. 2. I remember the love of thine *e.*

ESPOUSED

[Three-paragraph essay on meaning of term or on
its uses in the Scriptures, then:]

2 Sam. 3. 14. deliver me Michal which I *e.*

Mat.	1.	18.	when his mother Mary was *e.* to Joseph
Luke	1.	27.	to a virgin *e.* to a man named Joseph
	2.	5.	to be taxed with Mary his *e.* wife
2 Cor.	11.	2.	for I have *e.* you to one husband

Cotton-Newman (1658):

ESPOUSALS

| *Cant.* | 3. | 11. | crowned him in the day of his *espousals* |
| *Jer.* | 2. | 2. | I remember the love of thine *espousals* |

ESPOUSED

2 Sam.	3.	14.	deliver Michal which I *espoused*
Matt.	1.	18.	Mary was *espoused* to Joseph
Luke	1.	27.	a virgin *espoused* to a man
	2.	5.	taxed with Mary his *espoused* wife
2 Cor.	11.	2.	have *espoused* you to one husband

(4)

Cruden (1737):

GRASHOPPER, S.

Lev.	11.	22.	these ye may eat, the *g.* after his kind
Num.	13.	33.	and we were in our own sight as *g.*
Judg.	6.	5.	they came as *g.* for multitude, 7. 12.
Job	39.	20.	canst thou make him afraid as a *g.*
Eccl.	12.	5.	and the *g.* shall be a burden
Isa.	40.	22.	the inhabitants thereof are as *g.*
Jer.	46.	23.	because they are more than the *g.*
Amos	7.	1.	behold, he formed *g.* in the beginning
Nah.	3.	17.	thy captains are as the great *g.*

Cotton-Newman (1658):

GRASHOPPER

Lev.	11.	12.	these ye may eat, the *grashopper* after
Job	39.	20.	canst thou make him afraid as the *grash.*
Eccles.	12.	5.	and the *grashopper* shall be a burden

GRASHOPPERS

Num.	13.	33.	we were in our own sight as *grashopp.*
Judg.	6.	5.	they came as *grashoppers* for multitude
	7.	12.	they lay in the valley like *grashoppers*
Isa.	40.	22.	the inhabitants thereof are as *grashoppers*
Jer.	46.	23.	because they are more then the *grashopp.*

Amos   7. 1. behold, he formed *grash.* in the begin. of
Nahum   3. 17. thy captains as great *grashoppers*

(5)

Cruden (1737):

HALLOW

Exod.   28. 38. which children of Israel shall *h.*
           29. 1. to *h.* them to minister to me in the priests office
Lev.   22. 2. in those things which they *h.* to me, 3. 32. I am the Lord
                    which *h.* you
           25. 10. and ye shall *h.* the fiftieth year
Num.   6. 11. and he shall *h.* his head that same day
1 *Kin.*   8. 64. same day did king *h.* court. 2 *Chr.* 7. 7.
Jer.   17. 22. but *h.* ye the Sabbath-day, 24. 27.
Ezek.   20. 20. and *h.* my sabbaths, they be a sign
           44. 24. they shall keep laws and *h.* my sabbaths

Cotton-Newman (1658):

HALLOW

Exod.   28. 38. which the childr. of Israel shall *hallow*
           29. 1. to *hallow* them to minister
           40. 9. and shalt *hallow* the tabernacle
Levit.   16. 19. and *hallow* it from the uncleanness of
           22. 2. which they *hallow* unto me
                3. which the childr. of Isra. *hallow* unto the Lord
               32. I am the Lord which *hallow* you
           25. 10. ye shall *hallow* the fiftieth year and
Num.   6. 11. shall *hallow* his head that same day
1 *Kin.*   8. 64. same day did the king *hallow* the mid.
Jer.   17. 22. but *hallow* ye the sabbath day, as
               24. but *hallow* the sabbath day to do no work
               27. to *hallow* the sabbath day, and not to bear
Ezek.   20. 20. and *hallow* my sabbaths
           44. 24. and they shall *hallow* my sabbaths

(6)

Cruden (1737):

PALMS

1 *Sam.*   5. 4. both the *p.* of his hands were cut off
2 *Kin.*   9. 35. left but the skull and *p.* of her hands
Isa.   49. 16. graven thee on the *p.* of my hands

Dan.	10. 10.	which set me on the *p.* of my hands
Mat.	26. 27.	others smote him with the *p.* of their hands, Mark 14. 65.
Rev.	7. 9.	with white robes, and *p.* in their hands

Cotton-Newman (1658):

PALMS

1 *Sam.*	5. 4.	both the *palms* of his hands were cut
2 *King.*	9. 35.	and the *palms* of her hands
Isa.	49. 16.	graven thee on the *palms* of my hands
Dan.	10. 10.	and on the *palms* of my hands
Mat.	26. 27.	smote him with the *palms* of their ha.
Mar.	14. 65.	strike him with the *palms* of their ha.
Rev.	7. 9.	and *palms* in their hands

(7)

Cruden (1737):

TIMBREL

Exod.	15. 20.	and Miriam took a *t.* in her hand
Job	21. 12.	they take the *t.* and harp and rejoice
Psal.	81. 2.	take a psalm, bring hither the *t.*
	149. 3.	let them sing praises to him with the *t.*
	150. 4.	praise him with the *t.*, and dance

TIMBRELS

Exod.	15. 20.	women went out after her with *t.*
Judg.	11. 34.	his daughter came out with *t.*
2 *Sam.*	6. 5.	played before Lord on *t.* 1 *Chr.* 13. 8.
Psal.	68. 25.	were the damsels playing with *t.*
Jer.	31. 4.	thou shalt be adorned with thy *t.*

Cotton-Newman (1658):

TIMBREL

Exod.	15. 20.	Miriam—took a *timbrel* in her hand
Job	21. 12.	they take the *timbrel* and harp, & rejoyce
Psal.	81. 2.	take a Psalm, bring hither the *timbrel*
	149. 3.	sing praises to him with the *timbrel* & harp
	150. 4.	praise him with the *timbrel* and dance

TIMBRELS

Exod.	15. 20.	wom. went out after her with *timbrels*
Iudg.	11. 34.	his dau. came out to meet him with *ti*
2 *Sam.*	6. 5.	played before the Lord on *timbrels*

1 Chr.   13.   8.   played before G. with *timbrels* & cym.
Psal.   68. 25.   the damsels playing with *timbrels*

(8)

Cruden (1737):

UNDEFILED

Psal.   119.   1.   blessed are the *u.* in the way
Cant.   5.   2.   open to me my love, my dove, my *u.*
       6.   9.   my dove, my *u*, is one; she is the only one
Heb.   7. 26.   an high-priest, who is holy, harmless, *u.*
      13.   4.   marriage is honourable and the bed *u.*
Jam.   1. 27.   pure religion and *u.* before God
1 Pet.   1.   4.   to an inheritance incorruptible, *u.*

Cotton-Newman (1658):

UNDEFILED

Psal.   119.   1.   blessed are the *undefiled* in the way
Cant.   5.   2.   open to me—my dove, my *undefiled*
       6.   9.   my dove, my *undefiled* is but one
Heb.   7. 26.   who is holy, harmelesse, *undefiled*
      13.   4.   marriage is honourable & the bed *undefiled*
Iam.   1. 27.   pure religion and *undefiled* before G.
1 Pet.   1.   4.   to an inheritance incorruptible and *un.*

(9)

Cruden (1737):

UNICORN

[Preliminary essay on the nature of the unicorn and its use
in the Scriptures]

Num.   23. 22.   as it were strength of an *u.* 24. 8.
Job   39.   9.   will the *u.* be willing to serve thee
           10.   canst thou bind the *u.* in the furrow
Psal.   29.   6.   Lebanon and Sirion like a young *u.*
Psal.   92. 10.   shalt exalt like horn of an *u.*

UNICORNS

Deut.   33. 17.   his horns are like the horns of *u.*
Psal.   22. 21.   heard me from the horns of the *u.*
Isa.   34.   7.   the *u.* shall come down with them

Cotton-Newman (1658):

UNICORN

Num.   23. 22.   as it were the strength of an *unicorn*. Chap. 24. 8.

Job	39.	9. will the *unicorn* be willing to serve thee
		10. canst thou bind the *unicorn* with his han.
Psa.	29.	6. Lebanon & Syrion like a young *unico.*
	92.	10. shalt thou exalt like the horn of a *unicorn*

UNICORNS

Deut.	33.	17. his horns are like the horns of *unic*
Psal.	22.	21. heard me from the horns of a *unic*
Isai.	34.	7. the *unicorns* shall come down with me.

It will be seen in the examples above that Cruden sometimes adds an item, sometimes omits details from Newman, and occasionally makes a slight rearrangement. In his quoted matter he abbreviates the key words, as *c.* for *Colt,* and sometimes expands or reduces a sentence by a word or so. But, by and large, he follows his source closely, using the same references and the same order of appearance as Cotton-Newman and citing his Scriptural references in a perpendicular column before his contexts—a method which derived originally from the sixteenth century, as both authors were undoubtedly aware. The closeness of Cruden's adherence to Cotton-Newman is well illustrated in the last four examples—*Palm, Palms; Timbrel, Timbrels; Undefiled; Unicorn, Unicorns.* Examples from the separate concordances of the Apocrypha, such as *Feareth, Feast, Feathers,* reveal a similar relationship.

Among the authorities mentioned in the Preface to his first edition is Thomas Wilson (1563–1622), who published his *A Christian Dictionary* in 1612.[5] There were three subsequent editions. Although this dictionary is sometimes characterized as a concordance of the Bible, Wilson does not attempt to include all Biblical words but only those he regards of importance in elucidating doctrines and ideas in the Scriptures. Cruden knew this book and was perhaps attracted by its Calvinistic bias. Like a lexicographer of a later period, Wilson defines his terms and indicates by number (1, 2, 3, etc.) the various meanings of a word, citing Scriptural references in support of his conclusions, occasionally relating a history of the term. His method of procedure definitely anticipates the definition-essay passages employed by Cruden. In many items Cruden echoes or employs the actual phrasing of Wilson's

---

[5] See the sketch of Wilson in *DNB.* I have used copies of *A Christian Dictionary* printed in 1622 and 1630(?), now in the Humanities Research Center, The University of Texas.

text, as in *Book, Charity, Desire, Grace, Heaven, Joy, Justify, King-dom, Naked, Name*.[6] Other brief essays in Cruden, such as those on *Fox, Giants, Leopard, Lion, Mandrake, Pomegranate,* are based on accounts found in the early dictionaries.

In the Preface to his first edition Cruden refers to a number of his antecedents whose works he consulted but to whom he acknowledged no indebtedness. To one (possibly more) whose name is not listed he owes a small but definite debt. I refer to Robert F. Herrey and his "Two right profitable and fruitfull Concordances, or large and ample Tables Alphabeticall," published in 1578. The First Table, or alphabet, con-tained the Latin interpretation of proper names in the Bible—Hebrew, Chaldean, Greek, etc.—and the Second Table, an index, included all other important words. These tables, as printed after 1580 in the black-letter quarto Geneva Bibles, were regarded as a concordance. It is the First Table Alphabeticall that concerns us here. One small part of Cruden's magnum opus has the heading "An Alphabetical Table of the Proper Names in the Old and New Testament together with the Mean-ing and Signification of the Words in their Original Language." In his general Preface Cruden explains that he has divided his *Concordance* into three Alphabets, the first containing the common words, the sec-ond, the proper names (preceded by the Alphabetical Table), and the third, a concordance of the Apocrypha. He seems to be echoing Her-rey's two Tables Alphabeticall, and a sampling of entries reveals his use of Herrey's First Table.

But Herrey was not the only authority Cruden consulted in compiling his Alphabetical Table. He refers knowingly in his Preface to the work of Robert Stephens (i.e., Robert Estienne), naming especially the *Con-cordance* (*Concordantiae*) of 1555.[7] Though Cruden does not men-

---

[6] In Cruden's comments on *Elect, Election, Minister, Pastor, Predestinate, Reprobate* are echoes of the Calvinistic bias in these terms as applied in Wilson.

[7] *Concordantiae Bibliorum Vtriusque Testamenti, Veteris & Noui, nouae & integrae.* "Oliva Rob. Stephani. M. D. LV." I have used photostats and xerox copies of various openings from a copy in the University of Illinois Library. Among the entries in Estienne's *Concordantiae* which illustrate the author's methods and anticipate the English concordances are *Genu, Genua* (Knees); *Homo* (Man); *Ren* (Reins); *Remissio* (Remission); *Unicorn; Uxor* (Wife); *Vulpes* (Foxes); *Zelus* (Zeal); *Zona* (Girdle). Though keyed to the Vulgate Bible, Estienne's *Concordantiae* is comprehensive. It records all words

tion Estienne's proper-name Biblical glossary of 1537—the *Hebraea
. . . nomina*—the examples which follow reveal his familiarity with
this book as well as with Herrey's Concordance.

(1)

Cruden (1737):

ABILENE, the father of the apartment, or of mourning. A province between
Libanus and Anti-Libanus, whereof Lysanias was tetrarch. Luke 3. 1.

Herrey (1578):

Abilene. weeping, or crying, or lamentable, or the sonne of a Mansion, or
murmuring. A country whereof Lysanias was Tetrarch. Luke 3. 1.

Estienne (1537):

Abilina, Lugens vel plorans, siue pater māsiones vel murmurationis. D.
Nomen regionis, cui praeerat Lysias ā Romanis constitutus. luc. 3. a.

(2)

Cruden (1737):

ACHBOR, a rat; otherwise, bruising or enclosing, the well. He was father
of Baal-hanan, the seventh king of Edom. Gen. 36. 38.

Herrey (1578):

Achbar [marg. *Achobor*], *a mouse.* Father to Baal-hanan. Gen. 36. 38.
Chro. 1. 44.

Estienne (1537):

Achobar, Mus, vel conterens siue comprimens puteum. Filius Michai, 4 reg.
22. c. Pater item Balanam septimi regis in Edom, gen. 36. d.

(3)

Cruden (1737):

AGRIPPA. this word is Latin, and signifies one who at his birth causes
great pain, who is born with his feet foremost; *aeger partus.*

Herrey (1578):

*Agrippa. Sicke, sorrowful, grieved, or wearied, as one that is hardly de-
lieuered in childe-birth, or it is said to be he that in the birth putteth forth
his feet first of al.*

Estienne (1537):

Agrippa, Latinum est, dictum ab eo quod aegros, id est difficile partus faciat:
vel dicitur ille qui in nascendo prius emittit pedes.

---

in a single alphabet; it places all Scriptural references in perpendicular columns
before the phrase or sentence quoted for illustration; and it establishes the
precedent of making the references to book, chapter, and verse.

(4)

Cruden (1737):

BAAL-HERMON, the possessor of destruction; or of a thing cursed, devoted, or consecrated to God. It is a mountain. Judg. 3. 3.

Herrey (1578):

Baal-hermon, a possessour of destruction, or of a thing cursed, or dedicated, or consecrated, viz. *vnto God.* A hill. *Iudg.* 3. 3.

Estienne (1537):

Baal-hermon. Idolum aut author siue possessor destructionis, siue anathematis, vel retis, siue retiaculati, aut dedicati vel consecrati, deo scilicet. Mons circa Libanum in Palaesthinae finibus. iudic. 3. a

(5)

Cruden (1737):

BETHANY, the house of song, or of affliction; otherwise, the house of obedience, or the house of the grace of the Lord.

Herrey (1578):

Bethania, the house of obedience, or of affliction, or a house of a song, or of the grace of the Lorde

Estienne (1537):

Bethania, Domus obedientiae vel afflictionis, aut domus cantici, siue domus gratiae domini . . .

(6)

Cruden (1737):

CANAAN, a merchant, a trader. He was the son of Ham, and gave name to the land of Canaan. The Canaanites were a wicked people, for they descended from a wicked father, Gen. 13. 7.[8]

Herrey (1578):

Canaan. a marchant. the sonne of Ham. Gen. 10. 6. of whom the countrey of Canann tooke name. Gen. 11. 31. & 12. 5. & 13. 12. . . . the Canaanites were a wicked people. Gen. 12. 6. & 13. 7 for they descended of a cursed father. Gen. 10. 15–18.

Estienne (1537):

Chanaan, Mercator, vel negotiator, siue cantritus, vel confractus, aut recte respondens, vel recte affligens. Filius Cham. Gen. 10. a.

(7)

Cruden (1737):

HANNAH, gracious, merciful, or taking rest. The wife of Elkanah, and mother of Samuel.

---

[8] The *Canaan* item is transcribed from the fifth edition of Cruden (1794).

Herrey (1578):

Hannah [marg. *Anna, Hannah*]. *mercifull, or taking rest, or gracious.* The wife of Elkanah. 1 Sam. 1. 2. She obtaineth of God a son.

Estienne (1537):

Anna. Gratioso, siue misericors, aut requiescens, vel donans. Altera vxor Elcanae, 1 reg. 1. a.

(8)

Cruden (1737):

HIRAM, exaltation of life; or their whiteness; or their liberty; or he that destroys or anathematizes.

Herrey (1578):

Hiram. the height of life. A king of Tyrus . . .

Estienne (1537):

Hiram. . . . Albedo eorum, siue foramen. vel libertas eorum, aut destruens, vel anathematizans.

(9)

Cruden (1737):

IAPHIA, which enlightens, appears, or shows; or what groans. The son of David. 2 Sam. 5. 15.

Herrey (1578):

Iaphia, making see, appearing, or lightening. Sonne of Dauid. 2 Sam. 5. 15. and 1 Chron. 3. 7.

Estienne (1537):

Iaphia, Illuminans, siue apparens, aut gemens. Filius David. 2 reg. 5. c.

(10)

Cruden (1737):

JEBUS, which treads under foot, or contemns. A city, the same as Jerusalem. Judg. 19. 10.

Herrey (1578):

Iebus. a treading under foote, or a tumbling, or rolling, or manger. Jerusalem so called. *Judg.* 10. 10.

Estienne (1537):

Iebus, conculcatis, aut volutatis, vel praesepium. Nomen ciuitas quae & Ierusalem dicitur, iosue 18. d. iudicium 19. c.

Of the examples presented, Cruden follows Herrey in *Baal-Hermon, Canaan, Hannah,* and probably in *Bethania,* since neither Cruden nor Herrey translates the Latin of Estienne (omitted here) which follows "domini." Estienne's *Hebraea . . . nomina* is the source of Cruden's

Achbor, Agrippa, Hiram, Iaphia, Jebus (Iebus). In all of these, Cruden very likely consulted both Estienne's original Latin, the basis of Herrey's work, and Herrey's Concordance, but for the "Concordance of the Proper Names" as distinguished from the preceding "Alphabetical Table," Cruden depended solely on his major source, the Cotton-Newman *Concordance*.

Let it be emphasized here that Alexander Cruden originated very little of his immense mass of materials, including choice of words, contexts in which they were employed, Scriptural references and the method of citing them, the fairly numerous definitions and numbered meanings and descriptions or historical essays, and the meanings of the proper names in their original languages. All these things he found in work done by his predecessors. For what Cruden terms "Appellatives or Common Words" (the major portion of his *Concordance*), for the concordance of proper names (not their primitive meanings), and for the concordance of words in the apocryphal books, he depended upon some edition of the Cotton-Newman *Concordance* as his major source of information and method. Minor sources were Thomas Wilson's *Christian Dictionary*, Robert F. Herrey's Tables Alphabeticall, and Robert Estienne's *Hebraea . . . nomina*.

These conclusions concerning the provenience of Cruden's *Concordance* derive from an analysis of the first edition of his text (1737–1738) and a comparison with his antecedents. For twenty-five years the first edition was the Cruden in circulation—a text which contemporary students of concordances must have known was derived largely from the Cotton-Newman *Concordance*, some copies of which were still in circulation. What of Cruden's second and third editions, all published in his lifetime? Do these show any far-reaching changes which might enhance the worth and the vogue of his book?

In the Preface to the second edition of his *Concordance* Cruden writes:

The filling up of the lines to make the text fuller could not so well be done in the manuscript copy as in the printed. This renders the sentences more complete, in many thousands of places . . . some texts are added, and some improvements are made in the signification of words [that is, in the brief Alphabetical Table of the Proper Names].

A comparison of the texts of the first and second editions of the *Concordance* supports, in part, the author's claim, if allowance is made for his exaggeration of "in many thousands of places." With the printed text of the first edition before him, the author could see at a glance which Scriptural quotations illustrating the appearance of the head word did not fill up the printed lines. To fill a line he needed only to add a word or phrase from the Biblical context, being careful not to let the line run over. In thus "filling up the lines," a simple mechanical procedure, he made the principal additions to the second edition. A comparison of corresponding pages herein reproduced from the first (1737) and the second (1761) editions reveals clearly Cruden's procedure. Nine short sentences, shown on the facsimile pages of the 1737 edition, are "filled up," as shown on the corresponding facsimile pages of the 1761 edition. The pages thus terminate in the same way, retaining even the same catchword at the bottom right-hand corner; and this is characteristic throughout. No other changes are made in the main body of the *Concordance*; all the preliminary comment or brief essays or definitions, as in *Time,* remain the same. In the "Alphabetical Table of Proper Names" (8 pages out of a total of 719 in the 1958 edition) the author expands some items, as shown in three entries on the accompanying facsimile pages entitled "An Alphabetical Table of the Proper Names . . ." The few expansions or additions in the proper-name list derive from Estienne's glossary and Herrey's Concordance.

The third edition of Cruden's *Concordance* appeared in 1769 "with some improvements," according to the author, but it was hardly more than a reprint of the second, and the fourth (1785) and fifth (1794) editions followed the second. In short, the text of this second edition contains the sum total of Cruden's contribution.

The makers of Bible concordances in the seventeenth and early eighteenth centuries were consciously following a sixteenth-century tradition as exemplified in John Marbeck's English *Concordance* of 1550 and Robert Estienne's Latin *Concordantiae* of 1555. Cruden knew the methods exemplified by these authors and paid tribute to them; he knew too that these methods were continued in Cotton-Newman.

William Gouge, in his address "To the Reader" in the 1658 edition of the Cotton-Newman *Concordance*, also recalls the work of Marbeck,

2 Sam. 18. 20. Joab said, thou shalt not bear t.
22. why wilt thou run? thou hast no t. ready
31. Cushi came, Cushi said, t. my lord the king
1 Kin. 2. 28. then t. came to Joab, and Joab fled
14. 6. for I am sent to thee with heavy t.
1 Chron. 10. 9. sent, to carry t. to their idols
Psal. 112. 7. he shall not be afraid of evil t.
Jer. 20. 15. cursed be the man that brought t.
— 49. 23. for they have heard evil t.
Ezek. 21. 7. that thou shalt answer, for the t.
Dan. 11. 44. t. out of the east shall trouble him
Luk. 1. 19. I am sent to shew thee these glad t.
8. 1. shewing the glad t. of the kingdom of God
Acts 11. 22. t. of these things came to the church
— 13. 32. and we declare unto you glad t.
21. 31. t. came to the chief captain of the band
Rom. 10. 15. that bring glad t. of good things
See GOOD.

TIE.
1 Sam. 6. 7. and t. the kine to the cart, 10.
1 Kin. 18. † 44. t. thy chariot, and get thee down
20. † 14. who shall t. the battle? he said, Thou
— Prov. 6. 21. and t. them about thy neck
TIED.
Exod. 39. 31. and they t. to it a lace of blue
2 Kin. 7. 10. no man there, but horses t. asses t.
Mat. 21. 2. ye shall find an ass t, Mar. 11. 2, 4.
Luk. 19. 30.
TILE.
Ezek. 4. 1. thou also, son of man, take thee a t.
TILING.
— Luk. 5. 19. they let him down thro' the t.
TILL.
Gen. 19. 22. do any thing t. thou be come thither
1 Sam. 22. 3. t. I know what God will do for me
2 Sam. 3. 35. if I taste bread t. the sun be down
2 Chron. 26. 15. he was helped t. he was strong
36. 16. wrath arose, t. there was no remedy
Ezra 2. 63. t. there stood up a priest, Neh. 7. 65.
9. 14. be angry with us t. thou hadst consumed us
— Job 14. 1. I will wait t. my change come
27. 5. t. I die || Isa. 22. 14. not purged, t. ye die
Psal. 10. 15. seek wickedness t. thou find none
Prov. 29. 11. wise keepeth it in t. afterwards
Eccl. 2. 3. t. I might see what was that good
Cant. 2. 7. stir not up my love,t. he please, 3. 5.
Isa. 5. 8. lay field to field, t. there be no place
62. 7. t. he establish, t. he make Jerusalem a
praise in the earth
Jer. 49. 9. destroy t. they have enough, Obad. 5.
52. 3. t. he had cast them out from his presence
Lam. 3. 50. t. the Lord look down from heaven
— Ezek. 28. 15. t. iniquity was found in thee
Dan. 4. 23. t. seven times pass over him
Hos. 5. 15. t. they acknowledge their offence
10. 12. t. he rain righteousness upon you
Mat. 1. 25. t. she had brought forth her first-born
5. 18. t. heaven and earth pass, one jot not pass
Luk. 12. 50. I am straitened t. it be accomplished
15. 8. doth not seek diligently t. she find it
19. 13. he said unto them, occupy t. I come
John 21. 22. if I will that he tarry t. I come, 23.
Acts 7. 18. t. another king arose, who knew not
23. 12. not eat, t. they had killed Paul, 14, 21.
Eph. 4. 13. t. we all come in the unity of faith
Phil. 1. 10. without offence t. the day of Christ
1 Tim. 4. 13. t. I come, give attendance to reading
Rev. 2. 25. that which ye have, hold fast t. I come
7. 3. t. we have sealed the servants of our God
15. 8. t. the seven plagues were fulfilled
20. 3. t. a thousand years should be fulfilled
See CONSUMED, MORNING, UNTIL.
TILL.
Gen. 2. 5. was not a man to t. the ground, 2. 23.
2 Sam. 9. 10. and thy servants shall t. the land
Jer. 27. 11. they shall t. it, and dwell therein
TILLAGE.
1 Chron. 27. 26. Ezri over them that were for t.
Neh. 10. 37. Levites might have the tithes of t.
Prov. 13. 23. much food is in the t. of the poor
TILLED.
Ezek. 36. 9. I am for you, ye shall be t. and sown

Ezek. 36. 34. and the desolate land shall be t.
TILLER.
Gen. 4. 2. but Cain was a t. of the ground
TILLEST.
Gen. 4. 12. when thou t. ground, it shall not yield
TILLETH.
Prov. 12. 11. he that t. land, shall be satisfied
28. 19. he that t. his land shall have plenty
TIMBER.
Lev. 14. 45. he shall-break down the t. thereof
1 Kin. 5. 18. so they prepared t. 1 Chron. 22. 14.
2 Chron. 2. 9.
15. 22. and they took away the t. of Ramah
Ezra 5. 8. and t. is laid in the walls
6. 11. let t. be pulled down from his house
Neh. 2. 8. that he may give me t. to make beams
Ezek. 26. 12. they shall lay the t. in the water
Hab. 2. 11. the beam out of the t. shall answer
Zech. 5. 4. shall consume it with the t. thereof
TIMBREL.
Exod. 15. 20. and Miriam took a t. in her hand
Job 21. 12. they take the t. and harp, and rejoice
Psal. 81. 2. take a psalm, bring hither the t.
149. 3. let them sing praises to him with the t.
150. 4. praise him with the t. and dance
TIMBRELS.
Exod. 15. 20. women went out after her with t.
Judg. 11. 34. his daughter came out with t.
2 Sam. 6. 5. played before Lord on t. 1 Chron. 13. 8.
Psal. 68. 25. were the damsels playing with t.
Jer. 31. † 4. thou shalt be adorned with thy t.
TIME.
This term is commonly taken for the measure of motion, or for the duration of any thing. It is also taken for opportunity, or the favourable moment of doing or omitting any thing, Eccl. 8. 5. A wise mans heart discerneth both time and judgment: He knows both what he ought to do, and what are the fittest seasons for doing it. Our Saviour says, in John 7. 6, 8. My time is not yet come; by which some understand, the time of his death; others, the season of his appearing publickly in the world; and others, the time of his going up to the feast of tabernacles: q. d. I know my time to go, when it will be most safe and proper for me. I shall be there sometime during the feast, but my time is not yet come. The time of the vengeance of God, is sometimes called the time of the Lord, the time of his visiting, Jer 50. 27, 31. Wo unto them, for their day is come, the time of their visitation.
To gain the time is mentioned in Dan 2. 8. I know of certainty that ye would gain the time. The magicians required a length of time that his desire of knowing might have passed away, or that the dream might have come into his memory. St Paul advises the faithful to redeem the time, because the days are evil, Eph. 5. 16. Time is redeemed, when we carefully embrace and improve all the occasions and opportunities which the Lord presents unto us for his glory, and the good of our selves and others; not suffering these seasons to be stolen from us, and lost by cares and thoughts about the world: And whereas we have lost and misimproved much time, we ought therefore to double our diligence, and do the more good in time to come.
King Ahasuerus consulted with the wise men who knew the times, Esth. 1. 13. That is, he advised with his counsellors that understood the history, the customs, the laws of the Persians. The knowledge of history is one of the principal qualifications for a Statesman. For how should he know the interest of his country, if he is ignorant of its times, revolutions, and remarkable occurrences? St Jerom has it in his translation, he consulted the Sages that were always near his person, according to the custom of kings. The Chaldee paraphrast will have it, that he consulted the children of Issachar, who were skilful in the knowledge of times and

seasons. This tribe is noted for their knowledge of the times, 1 Chron. 12. 32. Of the children of Issachar, which were men that had understanding of the times, to know what Israel ought to do. Some by this understand their knowledge of the stars, and of the several seasons and changes of the air; which might be of good use in husbandry, to which this tribe was addicted. Others think, that by this is to be understood their political prudence in discerning and embracing the fit seasons for all their actions.
Christ Jesus says to his Apostles, who asked him if he was soon to restore the kingdom to Israel? It is not for you to know the times and seasons, which the Father hath put in his own power, Acts 1. 7. They still thought that the kingdom of the Messiah was a temporal kingdom: But afterwards they were undeceived, and the holy Ghost, which they received at Pentecost, instructed them, that the complete kingdom of the Messiah, the renewing of all things, was not to take place before the end of the world, Acts 3. 20, 21. where St Peter, speaking to the Jews, calls this time, a time of refreshing, and the times of the restitution of all things. St Paul, in 1 Thes. 5. 1, 2. makes use of almost the same terms, in which our Saviour expressed himself to his Apostles, concerning his last coming. But of the times and seasons ye have no need that I write unto you: For ye know that the day of the Lord cometh as a thief in the night.
Time is put for a year. Seven times, that is seven years, Dan. 4. 16. An acceptable time, is the time of the favour, of the goodness, and of the mercy, of God, Psal. 69. 13. My prayer is unto thee in an acceptable time. I pray in a time of grace, I seek thee when thou mayst be found, in a good day, in the day of grace and mercy. The devils complained, Mat. 8. 29. that Christ was come to torment them before the time, that is, before the last judgment, at which the devils will be thrown for ever into the fire prepared for them. The fulness of time, is the time which God had appointed and predicted as the fittest season for the coming of the Messiah, Gal. 4. 4. The Psalmist says, Psal. 31. 15. My times are in thy hand, that is, the time of my life, how long I shall live; or, all the affairs and events of my life, are wholly in thy power, to dispose and order as thou seest fit.
Gen. 18. 10. according to the t. of life, 14.
24. 11. the t. that women go out to draw water
39. 5. from the t. he had made him overseer
47. 29. the t. drew nigh that Israel must die
Exod. 21. 19. only he shall pay for loss of his t.
Lev. 15. 25. beyond the t. of her separation
18. 18. a wife besides the other in her life t.
Num. 23. 20. the t. was the t. of first ripe grapes
26. 10. what t. the fire devoured 250 men
Deut. 16. 9. such t. thou put the sickle to corn
Josh. 10. 27. at the t. of the going down of the fun, 2 Chron. 18. 34.
42. and their land did Joshua take at that t.
Judg. 18. 31. all the t. house of God was in Shiloh
2 Sam. 7. 11. since the t. I commanded judges
11. 1. at the t. when kings go forth to battle
23. 8. eight hundred he slew at one t.
2 Kin. 5. 26. is it a t. to receive money and garm.
1 Chron. 9. 25. were to come from t. to t. with them
Ezra 4. 10. peace, and at such a t. 11. | 7. 12.
10. 13. people are many, and it is a t. of rain
Neh. 2. 6. when wilt thou return? and I set him a t.
Job 6. 17. what t. they wax warm they vanish
9. 19. if of judgment, who shall set me a t. to plead
15. 32. it shall be accomplished before his t.
22. 16. wicked, which were cut down out of t.
38. 23. which I reserved against the t. of trouble
39. 1. knowest thou the t. they bring forth, 2.
Psal. 32. 6. in a t. when thou mayst be found
37. 19. they shall not be ashamed in the evil t.
41. 1. the Lord will deliver him in t. of trouble

FIG. 6. An opening from Cruden's *Concordance* (1737). Nine lines are indicated which Cruden "filled up" in the 1761 edition (see Fig. 7).

2 Sam. 18. 20. Joab said, thou shalt not bear t. this day
22. why wilt thou run? thou haft no t. ready
31. Cushi came, Cushi said, t. my lord the king
1 Kings 2. 28. then t. came to Joab, and Joab fled
14. 6. for I am sent to thee with heavy t.
1 Chron. 10. 9. and set t. to their idols
Psal. 112. 7. he shall not be afraid of evil t.
Jer. 20. 15. cursed be the man that brought t.
—49. 23. for they have heard evil t. faint-hearted
Ezek. 21. 7. that thou shalt answer for the t.
Dan. 11. 44. t. out of the east shall trouble him
Luke 1. 19. I am sent to shew thee these glad t.
8. 1. shewing the glad t. of the kingdom of God
Acts 11. 22. t. of these things came to the church
—13. 32. and we declare unto you glad t. the promise
21. 31. t. came to the chief captain of the band
Rom. 10. 15. that bring glad t. of good things
See GOOD.

TIE.
1 Sam. 6. 7. and t. the kine to the cart, 10.
1 Kings 18. † 44. t. thy chariot and get thee down
20. † 14. who shall t. the battle? he said, Thou
—Prov. 6. 21. bind on thy heart and t. about thy neck

TIED.
Exod. 39. 31. and they t. to it a lace of blue
2 Kings 7. 10. no man there, but horses t. asses t.
Mat. 21. 2. ye shall find an ass t. and a colt with
her, bring them to me, Mark 11.2,4. Luke 19.30.

TILE.
Ezek. 4. 1. thou also, son of man, take thee a t.

TILING.
—Luke 5. 19. they let him down thro' the t. with couch

TILL.
Gen. 19. 22. do any thing t. thou be come thither
1 Sam. 22. 3. t. I know what God will do for me
2 Sam. 3. 35. if I taste bread t. the sun be down
2 Chron. 26. 15. he was helped t. he was strong
36. 16. t. the wrath arose, t. there was no remedy
Ezra 2. 63. t. there stood up a priest, Neh. 7. 65.
9. 14. be angry with us t. thou hadst consumed us
—Job 14. 12. all days will t wait t. my change come
27. 5. t. I die || Isa. 22. 14. not purged, t. ye die
Psal. 10. 15. seek his wickedness t. thou find none
Prov. 29. 11. a wise man keepeth it in t. afterwards
Eccl. 2. 3. t. I might see what was that good
Cant. 2. 7. stir not up my love t. he please, 3. 5.
Isa. 5. 8. that lay field to field, t. there be no place
62. 7. and give him no rest t. he establish, t. he
make Jerusalem a praise in the earth
Jer. 49. 9. destroy t. they have enough, Obad. 5.
52. 3. t. he had cast them out from his presence
Lam. 3. 50. t. the Lord look down from heaven
—Ezek. 28. 15. wast perfect t. iniquity was found in
Dan. 4. 23. t. seven times pass over him
12. 13. but go thou thy way t. the end be
Hos. 5. 15. t. they acknowledge their offence
10. 12. t. he rain righteousness upon you
Mat. 1. 25. t. she had brought forth her first-born
5. 18. t. heaven and earth pass, one jot not pass
Luke 12. 50. I am straitned t. it be accomplished
15. 8. doth not seek diligently t. she find it
19. 13. he said unto them, occupy t. I come
John 21. 22. if I will that he tarry t. I come, 23.
Acts 7. 18. t. another king arose, who knew not
23. 12. not eat, t. they had killed Paul, 14, 21.
Eph. 4. 13. t. we all come in the unity of faith
Phil. 1. 10. without offence t. the day of Christ
1 Tim. 4. 13. t. I come, give attendance to reading
Rev. 2. 25. that which ye have, hold fast t. I come
7. 3. t. we have sealed the servants of our God
15. 8. t. the seven plagues were fulfilled
20. 3. t. the thousand years should be fulfilled
See CONSUMED, MORNING, UNTIL.

TILL, Verb.
Gen. 2. 5. was not a man to t. the ground, 2. 23.
2 Sam. 9. 10. and thy servants shall t. the land
Jer. 27. 11. they shall t. it, and dwell therein

TILLAGE.
1 Chron. 27. 26. Ezri over them that were for t.
Neh. 10. 37. Levites might have the tithes of t.
Prov. 13. 23. much food is in the t. of the poor

TILLED.
Ezek. 36. 9. I am for you, ye shall be t. and sown

Ezek. 36. 34. and the desolate land shall be t.
Gen. 4. 2. but Cain was a t. of the ground

TILLEST.
Gen. 4. 12. when thou t. ground, it shall not yield

TILLETH.
Prov. 12. 11. he that t. land shall be satisfied
28. 19. he that t. his land shall have plenty

TIMBER.
Lev. 14. 45. he shall break down the t. thereof
1 Kings 5. 18. so they prepared t. and stones to build
the house, 1 Chron. 22. 14. 2 Chron. 2. 9.
15. 22. and they took away the t. of Ramah
Ezra 5. 8. t. is laid in the walls, work prospereth
6. 11. let t. be pulled down from his house
Neh. 2. 8. that he may give me t. to make beams
Ezek. 26. 12. they shall lay thy t. in the water
Hab. 2. 11. the team out of the t. shall answer
Zech. 5. 4. it shall consume it with the t. thereof

TIMBREL.
Exod. 15. 20. and Miriam took a t. in her hand
Job 21. 12. they take the t. and harp, and rejoice
Psal. 81. 2. take a psalm, bring hither the t.
149. 3. let them sing praises to him with the t.
150. 4. praise him with the t. and dance

TIMBRELS.
Exod. 15. 20. all the women went out after her with t.
Judg. 11. 34. his daughter came out with t.
2 Sam. 6. 5. played before the Lord on t. 1 Chron. 13. 8.
Psal. 68. 25. were the damsels playing with t.
Jer. 31. † 4. thou shalt be adorned with thy t.

TIME.
This term is commonly taken for the measure of
motion, or for the duration of any thing. It
is also taken for opportunity, or the favourable
moment of doing or omitting any thing, Eccl.
8. 5. A wise man's heart discerneth both time
and judgment: He knows both what he ought
to do, and what are the fittest seasons for doing
it. Our Saviour says, in John 7. 6, 8. My
time is not yet come; by which some understand, the time of his death; others, the season of his appearing publicly in the world;
and others, the time of his going up to the
feast of tabernacles: that is, I know my time
to go, when it will be most safe and proper for
me. I shall be there sometime during the feast,
but my time is not yet come. The time of
the vengeance of God, is sometimes called the
time of the Lord, the time of his visiting, Jer.
50. 27, 31. Wo unto them, for their day is
come, the time of their visitation.
To gain the time is mentioned in Dan. 2. 8. I
know of certainty that ye would gain the
time. The magicians required a length of time
from the king to explain his dream, hoping
that his desire of knowing might have passed
away, or that the dream might have come into
his memory. St. Paul advises the faithful to
redeem the time, because the days are evil,
Eph. 5. 16. Time is redeemed, when we
carefully embrace and improve all the occasions
and opportunities which the Lord presents unto
us for his glory, and the good of ourselves
and others; not suffering these [seasons] to be stolen
from us, or lost by cares and thoughts about the
world: and whereas we have lost and misimproved much time, we ought therefore to double
our diligence, and do the more good in time to
come.
King Ahasuerus consulted with the wise men who
knew the times, Esth. 1. 13. That is, he advised with his counsellors that understood the
history, the customs, the laws of the Persians.
The knowledge of history is one of the principal qualifications of a Statesman. For how
should he know the interest of his country, if
he is ignorant of its times, revolutions, and
remarkable occurrences? St. Jerom has it in
his translation, he consulted the Sages that were
always near his person, according to the custom
of kings. The Chaldee paraphrast will have
it, that he consulted the children of Issachar,
who were skilful in the knowledge of times and

seasons. This tribe was noted for their knowledge
of the times, 1 Chron. 12. 32. Of the children
of Issachar, which were men that had understanding of the times, to know what Israel
ought to do. Some by this understand their knowledge of the stars, and of the several seasons
and changes of the air; which might be of
good use in husbandry, to which this tribe
was addicted. Others think, that by this is to
be understood their political prudence in discerning and embracing the fit seasons for all their
actions.
Christ Jesus says to his Apostles, who asked him if
he was soon to restore the kingdom to Israel? It
is not for you to know the times and seasons,
which the Father hath put in his own power,
Acts 1. 7. They still thought that the kingdom
of the Messiah was a temporal kingdom: But
afterwards they were undeceived, and the holy
Ghost, which they received at Pentecost, instructed them, that the complete kingdom of the Messiah, the renewing of all things, was not to take
place before the end of the world, Acts 3. 20, 21.
where St. Peter, speaking to the Jews, calls
this time, a time of refreshing, and the time
of the restitution of all things. St. Paul, in
1 Thess. 5. 1, 2. makes use of almost the same
terms, in which our Saviour expressed himself to his Apostles, concerning his last coming.
But of the times and seasons ye have no need
that I write unto you: For ye know that
the day of the Lord cometh as a thief in the
night.
Time is put for a year. Seven times, that is
seven years, Dan. 4. 16. An acceptable time,
is the time of the favour, of the goodness, and of
the mercy of God, Psal. 69. 13. My prayer
is unto thee in an acceptable time. I pray in a
time of grace; I seek thee when thou mayst be
found, in a good day, in the day of grace and
mercy. The devils complained, Mat. 8. 29. that
Christ was come to torment them before the time,
that is, before the last judgment, at which the
devils will be thrown for ever into the fire prepared for them. The fulness of time, is the
time which God had appointed and predicted
as the fittest season for the coming of the Messiah, Gal. 4. 4. The Psalmist says, Psal. 31.
15. My times are in thy hand, that is, the
time of my life, how long I shall live; or,
all the affairs and events of my life are wholly
in thy power, to dispose and order as thou
seest fit.
Gen. 18. 10. return according to the t. of life, 14.
24. 11. the t. that women go out to draw water
39. 5. from the t. he had made him overseer
47. 29. the t. drew nigh that Israel must die
Exod. 21. 19. only he shall pay for loss of his t.
Lev. 15. 25. if beyond the t. of her separation
18. 18. a wife besides the other in her life t.
Num. 13. 20. the t. was the t. of first ripe grapes
26. 10. what t. the fire devoured 250 men
Deut. 16. 9. such t. thou put the sickle to the corn
Josh. 10. 27. at the t. of the going down of the sun
Joshua commanded, 2 Chron. 18. 34.
42. and their land did Joshua take at one t.
Judg. 18. 31. all the t. the house of God was in Shiloh
2 Sam. 7. 11. since the t. I commanded judges
11. 1. at the t. when kings go forth to battle
—23. against eight hundred he slew at one t.
2 Kings 5. 26. is it a t. to receive money and garments
1 Chron. 9. 25. were to come from t. to t. with them
Ezra 4. 10. peace, and at such a t. 17. | 7. 12.
10. 13. people are many, and it is a t. of rain
Neh. 2. 6. when wilt thou return? and I set him a t.
Job 6. 17. what t. they wax warm they vanish
9. 19. if of judgment, who shall set me a t. to plead
15. 32. it shall be accomplished before his t.
22. 16. wicked, which were cut down out of t.
38. 23. which I reserved against the t. of trouble
39. 1. knowest thou the t. they bring forth, 2.
Psal. 32. 6. in a t. when thou mayst be found
37. 19. they shall not be ashamed in the evil t.
41. 1. the Lord will deliver him in t. of trouble

5 C 2   Psal.

FIG. 7. An opening from Cruden's *Concordance* (1761). Nine lines are indicated which Cruden "filled up" (compare with 1737 edition, Fig. 6).

An ALPHABETICAL TABLE of the PROPER NAMES in the OLD and NEW TESTAMENT:

Together with the Meaning or Signification of thefe Words in their Original Languages.

A.

AARON Signifies, Lofty, or mountainous; or, mountain of ftrength.
AARONITES.
ABADDON, The deftroyer.
ABAGTHA, Father of the wine-prefs.
ABANA, Made of ftone, or a building.
ABARIM, Paffages, or Paffengers; or furies.
ABDA, A fervant, or fervitude.
ABDI, He is my fervant.
ABDIEL, The fervant of God; or cloud of the abundance of God.
ABDON, A fervant or cloud of judgment.
ABED-NEGO, Servant of light.
ABEL, Adam's fecond fon, fignifies vanity, or breath, or vapour.
ABEL, A city, fignifies mourning.
ABEL-BETH-MAACHAH, Mourning to the houfe of Maachah.
ABEL-MAIM, The mourning of the waters; or the valley of waters.
ABEL-MEHOLAH, Sorrow or mourning of weaknefs, or of ficknefs.
ABEL-MIZRAIM, The mourning of the Egyptians.
ABEL-SHITTIM, Mourning of the thorns. It was a city near the Jordan in the wildernefs, Num. 33. 49.
ABEZ, An egg, or muddy. A city in the tribe of Iffachar, Jofh. 19. 20.
ABI, My father. The mother of Hezekiah, 2 Kin. 18. 2.
ABIAH, The Lord is my father; or the father of the Lord.
ABI-ALBON, Moft intelligent father, or the father over the building; or father of injury.
ABIATHAR, Excellent father, or father of him that furvived.
ABIB, Green fruits, or ears of corn.
ABIDAH, The father of knowledge, or the knowledge of the father. One of the fons of Midian, Gen. 25. 4.
ABIDAN, Father of judgment, or my father is judge.
ABIEL, God my father, or my God the father. He was the father of Kifh, 1 Sam. 9. 1.
ABIEZER, Father of help, or help of the father, or my father is my help.

ABI-EZRITE.
ABIGAIL, Father of joy, or the joy of the father.
ABIHAIL, The father of ftrength, or father of trouble.
ABIHU, He is my father, or his father.
ABIJAH, The will of the Lord, or the Lord is my father.
ABIJAM, Father of the fea.
ABILENE, The father of the apartment, or of mourning. A province between Libanus and Antilibanus, whereof Lyfanias was tetrarch, Luk. 3. 1.
ABIMAEL, A father fent from God, or my father comes from God. He was the fon of Joktan, Gen. 10. 28.
ABIMELECH, Father of the king, or my father the king.
ABINADAB, Father of willingnefs; or my father is a prince.
ABINOAM, Father of beauty or comelinefs; or my father is beautiful.
ABIRAM, A high father, or father of fraud.
ABISHAG, Ignorance of the father, or my father has feized, has taken, is arrived.
ABISHAI, The prefent of my father, or the father of the prefent; otherwife, The father of the facrifice, or the facrifice of my father.
ABISHALOM, The father of peace, or the peace of the father; or the recompenfe of the father. 1 Kin. 15. 2.
ABISHUA, Father of falvation, or of magnificence, or the falvation of my father. 1 Chron. 6. 4.
ABISHUR, The father of the wall, or of uprightnefs; or my father is upright. 1 Chron. 2. 28.
ABITAL, The father of the dew; or the father of the fhadow, according to the Syriack. One of David's wives, 2 Sam. 3. 4.
ABITUB, Father of goodnefs, or my father is good. 1 Chron. 8. 11.
ABIUD, Father of praife, or the glory of my father.
ABNER, Father of light, or the lamp of the father, or the fon of the father.
ABRAM, An high father; the father of elevation.
ABRAHAM, The father of a great multitude.
ABSALOM, Father of peace, or the peace of the father.
ACCAD, A veffel, a pitcher; or a fparkle.

The city where Nimrod reigned, Gen. 10. 10.
ACCHO, Clofe, inclofed, preffed together.
ACELDAMA, The field of blood. Acts 1. 19.
ACHAIA, Grief, or trouble.
ACHAICUS, A native of Achaia.
ACHAN, or ACHAR, He that troubles and bruifes.
ACHBOR, A rat; otherwife, bruifing or inclofing the well. He was father of Baal-hanan, the feventh king of Edom, Gen. 36. 38.
ACHIM, Preparing, confirming, or revenging.
ACHISH, Thus it is; or how is this?
ACHMETHA, A city.
ACHOR, Trouble.
ACHSAH, Adorned; or burfting of the veil.
ACHSHAPH, Poifon, tricks; or one that breaks; or the lip or brim of any thing.
ACHZIB, Liar, lying; or that runs; or that delays.
ADADAH, The witnefs or teftimony of the affembly. The name of a city, Jofh. 15. 22.
ADAH, An affembly. The wife of Lamech, Gen. 4. 19. Alfo the wife of Efau, Gen. 36. 2.
ADAIAH, The witnefs of the Lord. The father of Jedidah mother of Jofiah, 2 Kin. 22. 1.
ADALIAH, One that draws water; or poverty, or cloud, vapour, death. One of Haman's fons, Efth. 9. 8.
ADAM, The name of the firft man, Earthy man, red, of the colour of blood.
ADAMAH, Red earth; or of blood. A city, Jofh. 19. 36.
ADAMI, My man, red, earthy, human. A city, Jofh. 19. 33.
ADAR, High, or eminent.
ADBEEL, A vapour, a cloud of God; otherwife, A vexer of God. One of Ifhmael's fons, Gen. 25. 13.
ADDI, My witnefs, adorned, paffage, prey.
ADDON, Bafis, foundation, the Lord. It feems to be the name of a place, Neh. 7. 61.
ADIEL, The witnefs of the Lord. 1 Chron. 4. 36.
ADIN, Adorned, or voluptuous, dainty. Ezra 8. 6.
ADITHAIM, Affemblies, or teftimonies. Jofh. 15. 36.

ADLAI,

FIG. 8. First page of the proper-names section in Cruden's *Concordance* (1737). Three lines are indicated which Cruden "filled up" in the 1761 edition (see Fig. 9).

An ALPHABETICAL TABLE

OF THE

PROPER NAMES in the OLD and NEW TESTAMENT:

Together with the Meaning or Signification of the Words in their Original Languages.

Note, *There are some* PROPER NAMES *in this* TABLE, *which are not in the following Part of the* CONCORDANCE, *being seldom mentioned in Scripture.* To these the Place, where they are found, is annexed.

A.

AARON *signifies* lofty, *or* mountainous; *or* mountain of strength; *or* a teacher *or* teaching. *The son of* Amram, *brother to* Moses. *He was, with his sons, anointed and consecrated to the priest's office,* Lev. 8.

AARONITES.

ABADDON, the destroyer.

ABAGTHA, father of the wine-press.

ABANA, made of stone, *or* a building.

ABARIM, passages, *or* passengers.

ABDA, a servant, *or* servitude.

ABDI, he is my servant.

ABDIEL, the servant of God; *or* cloud of the abundance of God.

ABDON, a servant *or* cloud of judgment.

ABED-NEGO, servant of light.

ABEL, Adam's second son, *signifies* vanity, *or* breath, *or* vapour.

ABEL, *a city, signifies* mourning.

ABEL-BETH-MAACHAH, mourning to the house of *Maachah.*

ABEL-MAIM, the mourning of the waters; *or* the valley of waters.

ABEL-MEHOLAH, sorrow *or* mourning of weakness, *or* of sickness.

ABEL-MIZRAIM, the mourning of the *Egyptians.*

ABEL-SHITTIM, mourning of the thorns. *It was a city near the* Jordan *in the wilderness,* Num. 33. 49.

ABEZ, an egg, *or* muddy. *A city in the tribe of* Issachar, *Josh.* 19. 20.

ABI, my father. *The mother of* Hezekiah, 2 *Kings* 18. 2.

ABIAH, the Lord is my father, *or* the father of the Lord.

ABI-ALBON, most intelligent father, *or* the father over the building; *or* father of injury.

ABIATHAR, excellent father, *or* father of him that survived.

ABIB, green fruits, *or* ears of corn.

ABIDAH, the father of knowledge, *or* the knowledge of the father. *One of the sons of* Midian, *Gen.* 25. 4.

ABIDAN, father of judgment, *or* my father is judge.

ABIEL, God my father, *or* my God the father. *He was the father of* Kish, 1 *Sam.* 9. 1.

ABIEZER, father of help, *or* help of the father, *or* my father is my help.

ABI-EZRITE.

ABIGAIL, father of joy, *or* the joy of the father.

ABR

ABIHAIL, the father of strength, *or* father of trouble.

ABIHU, he is my father, *or* his father.

ABIJAH, the will of the Lord, *or* the Lord is my father.

ABIJAM, father of the sea.

ABILENE, the father of the apartment, *or* of mourning. *A province between* Libanus *and* Antilibanus, *whereof* Lysanias *was tetrarch,* Luke 3. 1.

ABIMAEL, a father sent from God, *or* my father comes from God. *He was the son of* Joktan, *Gen.* 10. 28.

ABIMELECH, father of the king, *or* my father the king.

ABINADAB, father of willingness; *or* my father is a prince.

ABINOAM, father of beauty, *or* comeliness; *or* my father is beautiful.

ABIRAM, a high father, *or* father of fraud.

ABISHAG, ignorance of the father.

ABISHAI, the present of my father, *or* the father of the present; *otherwise,* the father of the sacrifice, *or* the sacrifice of my father.

ABISHALOM, the father of peace, *or* the peace of the father; *or* the recompence of the father. 1 *Kings* 15. 2.

ABISHUA, father of salvation, *or* of magnificence, *or* the salvation of my father. 1 *Chron.* 6. 4.

ABISHUR, the father of the wall, *or* of uprightness; *or* my father is upright. 1 *Chron.* 2. 28.

ABITAL, the father of the dew; *or* the father of the shadow, *according to the* Syriac. *One of* David's *wives,* 2 Sam. 3. 4.

ABITUB, father of goodness, *or* my father is good. 1 *Chron.* 8. 11.

ABIUD, father of praise, *or* glory of my father.

ABNER, father of light, *or* the lamp of the father, *or* the son of the father.

ABRAM, an high father; the father of elevation.

ABRAHAM, the father of a great multitude. *At the command of God he goeth out of* Ur *of the* Chaldees *his native country into* Canaan, *where the Lord promised to give that land to his seed. The Messiah was promised to be of his family, for in his seed all the families of the earth were to be blessed,* Gen. 12. 3. Acts 3. 25. Gal. 3. 8. *He was circumcised with all his houshold, and taught his family to keep the commands of God. His faith was tried in being commanded to offer up his son* Isaac; *but the angel of the Lord stayed him, and* Isaac *was exchanged with a ram.* Isaac *in this matter was an eminent type and figure of* Christ, *who in the time appointed by God, was to*

ADA

be offered up a sacrifice for the sins of those that believe in him. The spiritual children of faithful Abraham, *are those that believe in* Jesus Christ, *and do the works of* Abraham, John 8. 39. Rom. 4. 16. and 9. 7. Gal. 3. 7, 22.

ABSALOM, father of peace, *or* the peace of the father.

ACCAD, a vessel, a pitcher; *or* a sparkle. *The city where* Nimrod *reigned,* Gen. 10. 10.

ACCHO, close, inclosed, pressed together.

ACELDAMA, the field of blood, *Acts* 1. 19.

ACHAIA, grief, *or* trouble.

ACHAICUS, a native of *Achaia.*

ACHAN, *or* **ACHAR,** he that troubles and bruises.

ACHBOR, a rat; *otherwise,* bruising *or* inclosing the well. *He was father of* Baal-hanan, *the seventh king of* Edom, Gen. 36. 38.

ACHIM, preparing, confirming, *or* revenging.

ACHISH, thus it is; *or* how is this?

ACHMETHA, *a city.*

ACHOR, trouble.

ACHSAH, adorned; *or* bursting of the veil.

ACHSHAPH, poison, tricks; *or* one that breaks; *or* the lip or brim of the city.

ACHZIB, liar, lying; *or* that runs; *or* that delays.

ADADAH, the witness *or* testimony of the assembly. *The name of a city,* Josh. 15. 22.

ADAH, an assembly. *The wife of* Lamech, *Gen.* 4. 19. *Also the wife of* Esau, *Gen.* 36. 2.

ADAIAH, the witness of the Lord. *The father of* Jedidah *mother of* Josiah, 2 *Kings* 22. 1.

ADALIAH, one that draws water; *or* poverty, *or* cloud, vapour, death. *One of* Haman's *sons,* Esth. 9. 8.

ADAM, earthy, taken out of red earth. *The name of the first man, who was made after the image of God in a holy and happy estate, but by his fall and disobedience broke covenant with God, and thereby brought himself and all his posterity into an estate of sin and misery,* Rom. 5. 12. *But* Jesus Christ *the second* Adam *is the Saviour and Redeemer of all that truly believe in him,* Mark 16. 16. Acts 4. 12. and 16. 31.

ADAMAH, red earth. *A city,* Josh. 19. 36.

ADAMI, my man, red, earthy, human. *A city,* Josh. 19. 33.

ADAR, high, *or* eminent.

5 Q 2
ADBEEL.

FIG. 9. First page of the proper-names section in Cruden's *Concordance* (1761). Three lines are indicated which Cruden "filled up" (compare with 1737 edition, Fig. 8).

and speaks in glowing terms of the labors of the Estiennes ("Stephens," as he terms them). Gouge[9] writes:

> But among others, the Stephens, Robert and Henry, has gone beyond all in skill and pains; insomuch as their Concordances, especially the last of Henry Stephens [a Greek concordance] justly bear this title, *Maximae & Absolutissimae Concordantiae*, the largest and perfectest concordances. Robert Stephens, the father, most diligently searched out all the words of Holy Scripture and set them down in an Alphabetical order, more full than ever before.

Gouge may have had in mind, particularly, Robert Estienne's Latin *Concordantiae*, but his remarks apply also to Robert's glossary and index prepared for editions of his *Biblia* and published as his *Hebraea . . . nomina* in 1537.

Although Marbeck's English *Concordance* and Estienne's Latin *Concordantiae* are similar in method and content, it would be difficult to prove that either copied the other. Marbeck's *Concordance* was published in 1550, and we know that his manuscript was in existence as early as 1542, when he was temporarily imprisoned for heresy. He could hardly have borrowed from the *Concordantiae* of 1555. Nor does it seem likely that Estienne would have converted Marbeck's English into Latin. The probabilities are that both imitated a fifteenth-century Latin concordance.[10] Whatever the sources, their concordances are similar in method. Both list all words (common words and proper names) in one alphabet—Estienne in Latin, with Latin lead words or

---

[9] I have found no information on the life of Gouge.

[10] John Marbeck (d. 1585), the first and most interesting of the English concordancers, was a theologian and musician, organist of St. George's Chapel, Windsor, and author of the first English concordance of the whole Bible (1550). In the Preface to his Concordance he states that the Latin words (used only in the headings) were those which "I founde in the Vulgate Latin Bible." Estienne's Latin *Concordantiae* was based also on the Vulgate. Some of the Vulgates had Latin concordances and could have been a common source. One such was *Biblia Latina*, published by Jean Petit in Paris, after 1493, to which a dozen leaves were added, entitled: *Biblia cum summariis concordantiis, divisionibus*, etc.

In the same Preface, Marbeck tells us his English words and phrases he "founde in the English Bible of the most allowed translacion." This was The Great Bible of 1539. The Herrey Concordance (1578) was keyed to the Geneva Bible, the Cotton-Newman and the Cruden to the King James Version.

headings, Marbeck in English with English and Latin lead words. Each centers the lead word above each group of references; each cites the Scriptural references in perpendicular columns before the quoted illustrations, as shown in the entries for *Foxe*, below.

Marbeck (*Concordance*, 1550):

FOXE
VULPIS

Iudic.	15.	a.	Samson caught three hundred foxes
1 *Esd.*	4.	a.	If a foxe go vp, he shall breake down
Psal.	62.	11.	that they may be a porciō of foxes
Cant.	2.	a.	Get vs she foxes, yea the lytle foxes
Thre.	5.	c.	the foxes runne vpon it
Ez.	13.	a.	thy Prophets are lyke the foxes vpon
Matth.	8.	c.	foxes haue holes and the byrdes haue nestes
Luke	9.	g.	as aboue
Luke	13.	g.	Go ye and tell that foxe

Estienne (*Concordantiae*, 1555):

VULPES

Iudicū.	15.	a. 4.	& cepit trecentes vulpes
Psal.	62.	c.11.	partes vulpium erunt
Cant.	2.	d.15.	capite nobis vulpes paruus
Thren.	5.	c.18.	vulpes ambulaverunt in eo
Ezec.	13.	a. 4.	quasi vulpes in deserto pp.
Matth.	8.	c.20.	vulpes foueas habent, &
Luc.	9.	g.58.	vulpes foueas habent, & v.
	13.	f.32.	ite, & dicite vulpi illi.

The glossing of the *Foxe* entry shows the system in vogue in Marbeck and Estienne. The same word in Cotton-Newman reveals continuation of the earlier methods; Cruden, following Newman, further exemplifies them.

Cotton-Newman (*Concordance*, 1658):

FOXES [Black-letter]

Iudg.	15.	4.	Samson went and caught 300. *foxes*
Psal.	63.	10.	they shall be a portion for *foxes*
Cant.	2.	15.	take the *fox*, little *fox*. that spoil the vine
Lam.	5.	18.	Zion desolate, the *foxes* walk upon it
Ezek.	13.	4.	thy prophets like *foxes* in desart

Mat.   8. 20. *foxes* have holes, birds have nests
Luke   9. 58. *foxes* have holes but the Son of man

Cruden (*Concordance*, 1737) :
FOXES

Judg.   15.   4. Samson caught three hundred *f.*
Psal.   63. 10. they shall be a portion for *f.*
Cant.   2. 15. take the *f.* the little *f.* that spoil
Lam.   5. 18. Zion is desolate, the *f.* walk upon it
Ezek.   13.   4. thy prophets are like *f.* in the desert
Mat.   8. 20. *f.* have holes, the birds nests, Luke 9. 58.

The glossing of *Foxes* (and there are thousands of other examples) reveals that a method which began in Marbeck and Estienne persisted in subsequent concordances to the time of Cruden. Estienne's *Concordantiae* was more extensive and more highly esteemed than Marbeck's work. To Estienne high tribute was paid by all, while Marbeck was mentioned with reservations. The *Concordantiae* was the great pattern for subsequent compilers and its system prevailed, as shown above, in the mass of Cruden's *Concordance*. Cruden's "Alphabetical Table of Proper Names" (not the concordance of these) shows that he also used Estienne's early glossary of proper names, *Hebraea . . . nomina* (1537), and its derivative, Herrey's "Tables Alphabeticall." Thus, analysis of Cruden's *Concordance* reveals that it was the consummation of a tradition which had as one of its earliest and most influential exponents the renowned Renaissance scholar, printer, lexicographer, Bible editor and commentator, and concordancer—Robert Estienne.

Although Cruden's *Concordance* was destined to have the widest vogue and most enduring popularity of all the concordances of the English Bible, the first edition showed little promise of the fame that was to follow after the author's death. It was almost twenty-five years before a second edition was printed, though Cruden does state in the Preface to the edition of 1761 that "several thousand" copies had been printed and "sold off" and a new edition had long been in demand. For the first two editions, he is said to have realized about £ 800.[11] The third, and last edition in Cruden's lifetime, appeared in 1769. A fourth edi-

[11] *DNB.*

tion was printed in 1785, a fifth in 1794, and other editions at intervals after the turn of the century (1805, 1810, 1833, 1845, etc.) until a thirty-sixth edition is recorded as of 1874 in the *British Museum Catalogue*. Concordances of Brown, Coles, and Eadie were only revisions of Cruden.[12] And the unabridged Cruden, still regarded as the best, is printed to the present day, as evidenced in the edition of 1958 by the Fleming H. Revell Company.

A statement in *A Religious Encyclopedia* (1887), edited by Philip Schaff, is prophetic. Having mentioned the English concordances from Marbeck to Newman, the writer concludes, "But all these attempts were forgotten on the publication by Alexander Cruden of his *Complete Concordance to the Holy Scriptures* . . . 1737. This work is likely to keep its place as the best of all the concordances as long as the King James version remains in use."[13] For more than seventy-five years since this utterance Cruden's *Concordance* has held its place and bids fair to continue to do so for a long period of time.

In the light of the provenience of the text it is not easy to understand why Cruden won a vogue and influence unheard of among his predecessors. I suggest the following explanations:

1) A happy rearrangement of conventional materials found in the Cotton-Newman *Concordance* and its antecedents in the sixteenth and seventeenth centuries. One example is Cruden's placing the proper names in an independent alphabet and stating their primitive meanings.

2) A reintroduction of certain practices from the earlier Bible scholars, such as the use of the definition and numbered meanings from Thomas Wilson's *Christian Dictionary,* and the meanings of proper names in the original languages from Estienne's *Hebraea . . . nomina* and Herrey's "Table Alphabeticall."

3) The manner of printing. The Cotton-Newman text, Cruden's important, immediate antecedent, was in thick folio, with black-letter

---

[12] *Schaff-Herzog Encyclopedia of Religious Knowledge* (III, 209) states: "Cruden's *Concordance* came out in 1737 and has often been republished in various forms, for example, by John Butterworth, Philadelphia, 1867; John Brown, London, 1866; C. S. Carey, London, 1867; John Eadie, New York, 1850; David King, Boston, 1845; Alfred Jones, London, 1855."

[13] Philip Schaff (ed.), *A Religious Encyclopedia,* I, 525.

headings. Cruden's work was in large quarto, in Roman type, with the headings or lead words in small capitals.

It is often not possible to account for the popularity of a book, but these are my suggestions as to why Cruden's *Concordance* has continued to lead all the rest in popularity and sales.

Estienne: Peter Oliver's
The Scripture Lexicon

THE CONCORDANCE which was derived from Robert Estienne and prepared for the Geneva Bible extended its influence into the eighteenth century. It was a major source for Peter Oliver's *The Scripture Lexicon* (1784).

Oliver himself was of more interest than his book. Of English descent, he was born in Boston in 1713 and graduated from Harvard University in 1730; he was appointed judge of the Inferior Court of Common Pleas at Plymouth in 1747, judge of the Superior Court in 1758, and chief justice in 1771. But he was a Loyalist, who had no sympathy with rebellion against constituted authority, and as differences between the colonists and England increased, Oliver's judicial duties became more difficult and dangerous. In 1776 he took up residence in England, where he was awarded a D.C.L. degree at Oxford and pensioned by the king. He lived at Birmingham until his death in 1791.[1] He left in manuscript perhaps his most interesting piece of writing—an account of "the origin and progress of the American Revolution."[2]

But we are concerned with his *The Scripture Lexicon*, published in Birmingham in 1784. The full title of this text is *The Scripture Lexicon, or a Dictionary of above Three Thousand Proper Names of Per-*

[1] For information on Oliver's life I am indebted to the article by James Truslow Adams in the *Dictionary of American Biography*, and the sketch by Clifford K. Shipton in *Sibley's Harvard Graduates*, VIII, 737–763.

[2] Published in 1961 as *Peter Oliver's Origin and Progress of the American Rebellion: A Tory View*. Edited by Douglas Adair and John Schutz.

sons and Places mentioned in the Bible. This lexicon obviously supplied a considerable demand in its day; besides the 1784 edition, other editions are recorded as of 1787, 1792, and 1797, and "new editions," 1810 and 1818.[3] Allibone lists a London edition as late as 1843. I find no evidence to support the statement in *DAB* that *The Scripture Lexicon* was used as a text at Oxford University.

The ultimate source of the proper names in *The Scripture Lexicon* is, of course, the Bible itself, but the work of assembling a vast body of materials is rarely the labor of a single compiler. He is likely to depend upon the industry of his predecessors for the accumulation of materials essential to his purpose. This procedure was followed by Peter Oliver in his making of *The Scripture Lexicon*. Although he nowhere mentions a specific author or book to which he is indebted, a statement in the Preface to the first edition of the *Lexicon* (repeated in later editions) suggests his knowledge of Herrey's Concordance. Herrey remarks, in the Preface to his Concordance, that he has placed together all the strange names and words from the Bible "remayning written in the Hebrew, Chaldean, Syrian, Greeke, or Latin language." With this we may compare Oliver's prefatory remark that "the meaning of most of the words is inserted according to the Hebrew, Chaldee, Syrian, Greek, Latin and other antient languages." Confirmation of his knowledge of Herrey's book is also amply established by his numerous borrowings.

The wording of the title page of the first edition of the *Lexicon,* stating that this is a "Dictionary of above Three Thousand Proper Names," may indicate that Oliver knew a late revision of Herrey's book, published about 1660, with the title *Scripture Names Expounded,* and limited to four thousand proper names.[4] The original Herrey Con-

----

[3] Editions of *The Scripture Lexicon* are listed by Allibone, Lowndes, and *Sibley's Harvard Graduates*.

Copies of the *Lexicon* are fairly scarce. I have used a copy of the first edition (1784) in Brown University Library; of the second edition (1787) in Harvard University Library; of the "new edition" of 1810 in the Boston Public Library; and of the 1797 edition, which was examined for me by Professor James Sledd in Mr. Elsdon C. Smith's private collection, Evanston, Illinois.

[4] The title page of *Scripture Names Expounded* reads, in part: "Containing the Interpretation of about foure thousand Proper Names . . . in the Hebrew, Caldean, Greeke, and Latine Tongues, dispersed throughout the Bible. Col-

cordance, printed in 1578, was in two parts: (1) "The First Table,"
consisting of about three thousand proper names (although no number
was mentioned); and (2) "The Second Table," consisting of common
nouns and substantives—key words to the more important actions.
Oliver seems not to have used the last Table. He may well have followed the lead of "S. D.," the 1660 reviser, in presenting only the
proper names. The comparative examples which follow come from the
first edition of *The Scripture Lexicon* (1784)[5] and the 1581 edition of
the Herrey Concordance. Oliver is wholly dependent on Herrey's Concordance for the first group.

(1)

Oliver: *Antilibanus (i.e. against Libanus)* An high hill to the north of
Judea opposite mount Libanus.

Herrey: *Antilibanus, for, or against Libanus.* A high hill on the northside
of Iudea agains Libanus.

(2)

Oliver: *Bathsheba* or *Bathsua (i.e. seventh daughter, or the daughter* of an
oath) The wife of Uriah, one of king David's generals, whom
David afterwards married.

Herrey: *Bathsheba, the seventh daughter, or the daughter of an othe.* The
daughter of Eliam, and wife of Uriah the Hittite. 2 Sam. 1.
3 . . . David causeth Uriah to be slaine, and afterwards married
her . . . She is called Bathsua, the daughter of Ammiel. 1 Chro.
3. 5.

(3)

Oliver: *Eleazer (i.e. the help, or aid of God)* The third son of Aaron the
high priest of the Jews—also others.

Herrey: *Eleasar, the helpe, or ayde of God,* sonne of Aaron, Exod. 6. 23 . . .
after Aarons death he became the hie Priest. Num. 20. 18. 5.
Deut. 10. 6. . . . also the sonne of Abinadad. 1 Sam 7. 1. Also
the sonne of Abaron . . . Also Iosephs great grandfather.

---

lected by R. F. H." For a fuller discussion of *Scripture Names Expounded,* see
Chapter III.

    [5] The Brown University Library copy. The words are printed in capitals, as,
for example, EA'-NAS, E'-BAL, E'-BED, E'-BED-ME'-LECH, EB-EN-EZ'-ER,
EB'-ER, EB-I'-A-SAPH, EB-RO'-NAH. We are not concerned with accentuation and so do not follow this method of listing the words.

(4)

Oliver: *Hosannah* (*i.e. save I pray thee, or keep or preserve I beseech thee, or give salvation*) A form of benediction made use of by the Jews, and particularly applied to Christ at his last entry into Jerusalem.

Herrey: *Hosanna, Saue I pray thee, or kepe, or preserue, I beseech thee, or giue saluation*. Psal. 118. 25. This prayer the people applied to Christ, at his last entrie into Ierusalem. Mat. 21. 9. Mar. 11. 9. 10.

(5)

Oliver: *Huldah* (*i.e. The world, circle of the world, or west*) A prophetesse, the wife of Shallum, to whom king Josiah sent for counsel.

Herrey: *Huldah, the world, circle of the world, or west*. A prophetesse, wife to Shallum. 2 Kin. 22. 14. to whom king Iosiah sent for counsell. 2 Chro. 34, 21 to 29.

The following seven successive entries in *The Scripture Lexicon* derive solely from the Herrey Concordance: *Hushah, Hushai, Husham, Hushathite, Hushim, Huzzab, Hydaspes.*

In the series of entries below, Oliver borrowed from the Concordance and supplied additional details from the Scriptural passages to which Herrey had made specific reference:

(1)

Oliver: *Bartimeus.* The name of a blind man mentioned by St. Matthew, the son of Timeus, *Bar* being the word for a son.[6]

Herrey: Bartimeus, Ierome sayth should be written *Barsemeus*, which in the Syrian tongue is interpreted, *blind sonne, or the sonne of blindnesse*, Of whom read Marke 10. 46 [etc.].

(2)

Oliver: *Parmashta* (*i.e. the breaking of a foundation, a bull of one year old*) The seventh son of Haman, who was hanged with his nine brethren, at the same time his father was.

Herrey: *Parmashta, the breaking of a foundation*: or after the Hebrue and Syrian, *a bull of one yeares age.* Est. 9. 9. [Oliver probably read Esther 9. 9–15.]

---

[6] Oliver obviously misread the "Marke" in the Concordance reference as "Matthew," and did not verify the Scriptural passage.

(3)

Oliver: *Pelaliah* (*i.e. thinking on the Lord, the judgment of the Lord*) A son of Amzi and father of Jeroham.

Herrey: *Pelaliah, thinking on the Lord, or the judgment of the Lord.* Nehe. 11. 12. [In Nehemiah, we read: ". . . and Adiah, the son of Jeroham, the son of Pelaliah, the son of Amzi."]

(4)

Oliver: *Rhoda* (*i.e. a rose*) A damsel convert of Christianity mentioned in the book of Acts.

Herrey: *Rhoda, a rose.* Acts 12. 23 [13?] [Acts 12. 13 reads: "And as Peter knocked at the door of the gate, a damsel came to hearken, named Rhoda."]

(5)

Oliver: *Terah* (*i.e. smelling, breathing, driving away*) the father of the patriarch Abraham, and the son of Nahor.

Herrey: *Terah. smelling, breathing, driving away.* Abrahams father. Gen. 11. 26. [Genesis 11. 24 reads: ". . . and Nahor liued nine and twenty years and begat Terah," and 11. 25 reads: ". . . and Terah liued seuenty years and begat Abram, Nahor, and Haran."]

In *The Scripture Lexicon* (1784) Peter Oliver almost always borrowed the primitive definitions of Hebrew proper names from the Geneva (Herrey) Concordance. From the same source, he frequently selected details to fill up his entry. The result is that many of Oliver's descriptions or explanations depend solely upon that Concordance. In other entries, the compiler re-enforced the primitive meanings found in his source by selecting concrete details from the Scriptural passages referred to by the Concordance. For a considerable number of entries, the author supplied dates from some Biblical chronology or chronologies. Such chronologies were current from the time of Eusebius Pamphilus in the fourth century to Scaliger, Reusner, Calvisius, Petavius, Helvicus, and Archbishop Ussher in the sixteenth and seventeenth centuries. Although Oliver might have found specific information in almost any of these as to dates (A.M., B.C., etc.) which he supplied for the patriarchs, the kings, and judges of Judah and Israel, there is reason to believe that he drew largely from two sources for his chronology. One source was a book published by Thomas Prince, an admired

Thomas Summaster.

CONCORDANTIAE BI-
bliorum vtriufque Teftamenti, Veteris & Noui, nouæ & integræ.

Quas re vera Maiores appellare poffis.

STEPHANVS TYPOGRAPHIS.

AEquos &innocuos vos præbete ὁμωτίχφ ὑμῶν, rogo atque obfecro.
PRIVILEIVM ipfi vltrò ad annos aliquot irrogate, vt meffi alienæ parcatis.
Cœpta, nedum expolita, meliora facere & perficere finite,
vobis in tempore profutura. 12.

OLIVA ROB. STEPHANI
M. D. LV.   ⅅ

FIG. 10. Title page of Robert Estienne's *Concordantiae* (1555).

contemporary of Oliver. Prince's book is entitled *A Chronological History of New England: In the Form of Annals* (1602–1730).[7] Of special interest for this study is the Introduction, containing an epitome, in graphic form, of the most remarkable transactions and events since the Creation, including the connected line of time, the succession of patriarchs and sovereigns of the most famous kingdoms and empires, the gradual discoveries of America, etc.

Prince's *Chronological History* was published by subscription, in Boston, in 1736. A long list of subscribers is printed in the beginning of the book, and prominent among their names is that of Peter Oliver, who is to take six copies. Oliver would have found in any one of his six copies these topics presented in chronological tables: (1) The Scripture Patriarchs, (2) The Judges of Israel, (3) The Kings of Judah, (4) The Babylonian, Persian, Grecian, and Egyptian Kings, (5) The Roman and Greek Emperors, (6) The Kings of England. The tables are so arranged that they may be read like a railroad timetable, and by reading across the page horizontally and observing the figures in the perpendicular column, one can readily find the alleged dates of birth, of rule, and of death, or length of life. Oliver knew and made use of Prince's annals, to which he was a heavy subscriber, as evidence to be presented below will show.

But certain features, such as the abbreviations A.M. (Anno Mundi), B.C., AEt. (AEtas), indicate that he also consulted other better known and more authoritative writers on chronology. Prince himself was a man of learning who frequently cited the chronologers on whom he depended. Among these were Helvicus, Petavius, Ussher, and others, the one most frequently cited in his footnotes being Helvicus. From his study of Prince's book, Oliver may well have been drawn to consult some of the authorities there cited, especially Helvicus. Christopher Helvicus (1581–1617), a German theologian and educator, first published his *Theatrum Historicum, sive Chronologiae Systema Novum* at Giessen in 1609. At least three other Latin editions were printed by 1662.[8] In 1687 an English translation was published in London: *"The*

---

[7] A copy of Prince's *Chronological History* (Volume I only) is in the Humanities Research Center, The University of Texas. My references are to this copy.

[8] See the sketch of Christopher Helvicus in the *Schaff-Herzog Encyclopedia*

Historical and Chronological Theatre of Christopher Helvicus. Faithfully done into English . . ."[9] In his day Helvicus was held in high esteem. About 1655 an English scholar-priest, compiling a list of books as "A Library for Younger Schollers," placed Helvicus first among his authorities: ". . . the most exact Chronologer in that kind . . . hee should allwayes be open before you."[10] It was not strange that Oliver should check Prince's *Chronological History* by reference to Helvicus.

As a generous subscriber to the *Chronological History,* Peter Oliver must have read this book carefully, and in compiling his *Scripture Lexicon,* he probably consulted Prince's work for the chronology of Biblical persons and places. In his tables, Prince places together the date of a patriarch's death and his age or number of years he had lived in the Year of the World, the date of birth having been set down earlier; for example, we read in the column: "Y. W. [Year of the World] 2096, *Arphaxad* dies, aged 438." Then, in a similar fashion, on the same page follow the names *Salah, Shem, Abraham, Eber, Isaac, Jacob* together with the Y.W. dates of death and the ages. This is the pattern which Oliver follows—the date of death and the age—and the numbers correspond to those given in Prince's table for the names listed above and many others. Oliver does not, however, use Y.W., Prince's heading for "Year of the World," but chooses A.M., found in other chronologies for "Anno Mundi," and AEt. for "AEtas" (age.).

In Helvicus, the authority most frequently cited by Prince, Oliver would have found precedent for his abbreviations and sometimes phrasing that he adapted. Oliver seems not to have followed the Helvicus pattern of placing together the A.M. date of birth and the number of years lived. Given this information he could readily estimate the date of death, of course; for example, if Helvicus states that "Eber was born A.M. 1723 . . . He lived 464 years," Oliver would need only to add the two numbers to determine the date of Eber's death as A.M. 2187. Prince's reasoning that Adam was not 130 until the beginning of the

---

of Religious Knowledge, and one by Watt in the *Bibliotheca Britannnica,* Volume I.

9 References to Helvicus are to a copy of the 1687 edition of *The Historical and Chronological Theatre* in my own collection.

10 *A Library for Younger Schollers,* edited by Alma DeJordy and Harris F. Fletcher, was published in 1961 by the University of Illinois.

Year of the World 131 (and that Noah's flood was in the Year of the World 1657, not 1656 as was generally reckoned) led to a discrepancy between Prince and Helvicus of one year in birth dates. Oliver sometimes followed Prince in the discrepancy, and sometimes corrected the dates by checking Helvicus, though generally he avoided the problem by omitting the birth date. The examples of chronological entries which follow will serve to point up the relationship of Oliver to his two sources.

(1)

Oliver: *Arphaxad* (i. e. *healing*) A son of the patriarch Shem, from whom the Chaldeans proceeded; he died A. M. [Anno Mundi] 2096. AEt. 438—also a king whom Nebuchadnezzar vanquished.

Herrey: *Arpachshad* [marg. *Arphaxad*] *healing.* The sonne of Shem. Gen. 10. 22. &c . . . Also a king whom Nabuchodonosor vanquished. Iudith. 7. 1.

Helvicus: *Arphaxad*, the Son of Sem, was born A. M. 1658 . . . He lived 438 years. [Under the heading, "The Age of Patriarch," p. 4.]

Prince: Y. W. 2096: Arphaxad Dies, Aged 438.

(2)

Oliver: *Cainan* (i. e. *possessor, or puchaser, or one who laments*) The son of Enos the patriarch, died A.M. 1235, AEt. 910.

Herrey: *Kainan* (Kenas) *A buyer, or owner.* Gene. 5. 9.

Helvicus: *Kenan* was born in the year of the World, and of Adam 325. of Enos 90. . . . He lived 910 years.

Prince: *Cainan.* Y. W. 1235: Cainan Dies, Aged 910.

(3)

Oliver: *Eber* (i. e. *passage or anger*) A descendant from the patriarch Shem, he died A. M. 2187, AEt. 464.

Herrey: *Eber* [Heber] *passing, passage, or anger.* The sonne of Selah. Gen. 11. 14.

Helvicus: *Eber* was born A. M. 1723 of Salah 30. Gen 11.v.14. He liv'd 464 years.

Prince: *Eber.* Y. W. 2187: Eber Dies, Aged 464.

(4)

Oliver: *Enos,* or *Enosh* (i. e. *fallen man, or desperation*) The son of Seth and father of Cainan, was born A. M. 235, died A. M. 1140, AEt. 905; his posterity were called the sons of God.

Herrey: *Enosh (Enos) man, or desperation.* The sonne of Sheth. Gen. 2, 46 . . . Enosh liued 905 yeeres. Gen. 5. 11.

Helvicus: *Enos* was born in the year of the World 235, of Seth 105. Gen. 5.v.6. He liv'd 905 years.

Prince: *Enos* Y. W. 1140: Enos Dies, Aged 905.

(5)

Oliver: *Methusael* or *Methuselah,* or La. (i.e. *he sent his death, the weapon of his death, the spoil of his death*) The son of Mehajael or Enoch, and father of Lamech; the longest liver upon record; he died A. M. 1656, AEt. 969.

Herrey: *Methushelah he sent his death, or the weapon of his death;* or after the Hebrue and Syrian. *Spoyling his death,* of *the spoyle of death.* The father of Lamech. Gen. 5. 25–27.

Helvicus: *Methusalah* was born A. M. and of Adam 687, of Enoch 65. He was the longest liv'd of all mankind, viz. 969 years. Gen. 5.v.21.

Prince: *Methusalah.* Y. W. 1656: Methusalah Dies, Aged 969.

The foregoing examples show:

1) In every instance Oliver's parenthetic matter derives from the Herrey Concordance, as do other details sometimes, i.e., *Arphaxad,* "Also a king whom Nebuchadnezzar vanquished."

2) Oliver tends to follow the usual pattern of Prince's *Chronological History,* placing together the date of death and the span of life, or age, instead of following Helvicus' practice of stating the date of birth and the years lived.

3) Oliver rejects Prince's abbreviation of Y.W. for "Year of the World," Y.L. for "Year of Life," and Y.C. for "Year of Christ." He has recourse to A.M. (Anno Mundi) for "Year of the World," as used by Helvicus and other chronologers.

4) Oliver sometimes corrects the birth date by reference to Helvicus; in *Enos,* for example, Oliver writes "A. M. 235," not "236," as does Prince. Likewise in the entry *Noah* (not listed above) Oliver gives "A. M. 1056" as the birth date, not "1057," as does Prince.

5) In the entry *Methusael* or *Methuselah,* Oliver's "the longest liver upon record" may be an echo of Helvicus' "He was the longest liv'd of all mankind."[11]

[11] The possibility that Oliver could have taken his A.M. dates from refer-

A major source for *The Scripture Lexicon* was undoubtedly Herrey's First Table of 1578. This source was supplemented by chronology drawn largely from Thomas Prince's *Chronological History* (1736) and Christopher Helvicus' *Historical and Chronological Theatre* (1687), and padded by many names not found in these sources and not always of great importance, though they were from the Bible. These names were supplied perhaps by Oliver himself or quite possibly were taken from an edition of Herrey assembled by a certain "S. D.," a seventeenth-century editor of the Herrey Concordance.[12]

In assembling the extra proper names, the compiler probably consulted passages in the Scriptures where many names are given, alphabetized them, wrote headings for them, and thus had them ready for use in his own comprehensive lexicon or dictionary. In the entry *Naashon,* for example, Oliver writes "*Naashon, or Nashon* . . . Aaron's brother-in-law, the son of Aminidab, a prince of the tribe of Judah." Oliver cites no Scriptural reference, but he is following Numbers 7: 12 ff.: "And he that offered the offering the first day was Nashon the son of Aminidab, of the tribe of Judah." As there were twelve princes making offerings, with the name of the prince, his father, and the tribe given in each case, we can see a concentration of 36 names (Numbers 7:12–78).

In a similar way, the author must have used other concentrations of names in the Bible. He undoubtedly noted the names, for example, in the genealogical passages, as in the generation of Adam (Genesis 5); the generations of Noah (Genesis 6) and of Noah's sons Shem, Ham, and Japheth (Genesis 10–11); the genealogy of Christ (Matthew 1, Luke 3); and the generation of the tribes of Israel and their families (Genesis 35, 36, 46; Exodus 1, 6; I Chronicles 2–9).

Among the recurring entries in *The Scripture Lexicon* is "One returned from the Babylonish Captivity." The person may not have had any further importance than that he returned. These names are all to

---

ence Bibles with dates indicated in the margins has been examined. In many English Bibles published after 1701 marginal dates supplied by Archbishop Ussher are B.C. and A.D. dates. Some Bibles printed at Oxford in the 1670's and 1680's (see Darlow and Moule) are said to have the A.M. dates in the margin. Oliver would have found it more economical, however, to borrow from the concise tables in Prince and Helvicus.

[12] See *"Scripture Names Expounded,"* Chapter III.

be found in Ezra 2, 7, 8. Since it was estimated that 42,360 souls returned from the captivity, not to mention 7,337 servants and maids and
200 singing men and women, Oliver had many to draw from, though,
of course, not all are listed. Under *A* he introduces 40 names of those
returned from the captivity.

Under the entry *Camp, or Encampment of the Israelites,* Oliver
lists the names of the forty-one camp sites of the children of Israel
when they were led out of Egypt. These names, drawn from Numbers
33, also are distributed in order in the alphabet. From Numbers 35
and Joshua 20:7–8 come the list of refuge cities noted by Oliver. Such
are the sources of *The Scripture Lexicon,* including some of the
methods of extending, even padding, the proper-name list.

The Scripture Lexicon states on the title page that it is a dictionary
of "proper names" of persons and places from the Bible, but the author
does in fact intersperse a great many entries of common nouns among
the proper names. Some of these are, for example, *acts, amethyst, anath-
ema, angel, beryl, chrysoprasus, hour, Passover, Refuge Cities.* These
additions extend the word list considerably, though they are hardly
Hebrew proper names, and they persist in subsequent editions. These
entries do not derive from the Second Table of Herrey's Concordance,
which is concerned with common nouns and substantives as key words,
but come probably from Biblical commentaries and other sources of
information.

My principal aim in this chapter has been to show that Peter Oliver's
The Scripture Lexicon is a compilation from sources unacknowledged
by him, and, so far as I know, hitherto undiscovered. A major source
undoubtedly was the Concordance ascribed to Robert F. Herrey and
published with the black-letter quarto editions of the Geneva Bible
from 1578 to 1615. This Concordance supplied nearly all primitive
meanings of the Hebrew proper names and records of Biblical events
with supporting Scriptural references, thus enabling the compiler
readily to find additional information by reading the cited passages in
the Bible. For the A.M. and B.C. dates of the patriarchs, Oliver seems
to have consulted principally two chronologies: Thomas Prince's
Chronological History (1736) and Christopher Helvicus' *Historical
and Chronological Theatre* (1687). For extension or padding of his
proper-name word list, Oliver, or a seventeenth-century reviser of

Herrey's Concordance, seems to have resorted to genealogical and tribal lists in Genesis, Exodus, Numbers, Joshua, Chronicles, and Ezra. He thus inflates his word list and includes some people whose names are of little or no importance in Jewish history. It is interesting to observe that the materials thus assembled continued in subsequent editions of *The Scripture Lexicon* (1787 and 1797) and, with almost no change, in the "new edition" of 1810.[13]

The second edition of the *Lexicon* in 1787—the last in Oliver's lifetime—shows certain revisions. For this edition the author claims four thousand words, or entries, as against three thousand in the 1784 text. The revised *Lexicon* incorporates in alphabetical order in the body of the text the considerable number of items contained in the Appendix of 1784; it employs brackets instead of parentheses to enclose the Hebrew primitive meanings, and inserts before each definition the Greek equivalent of the Hebrew.

The claim of expansion by a thousand words—that is, of proper Hebrew names—is hardly demonstrable. Three groups of entries chosen at random from the 1784 edition and the revision of 1787 reveal but slight increase in the proper-name entries. Between *Cab* and *Calvary,* for example, there are twenty-one entries in the 1784 text, twenty-seven in the 1787. From *Jehoiarib* to *Jehudijah,* twenty-two in each text; from *Rahab* to *Rapha,* sixteen in 1784, and seventeen in 1787. In short, a total of fifty-nine entries in the first edition had increased to only sixty-six in 1787. This seems typical. The wording in corresponding entries is generally the same. Perhaps the augmentation claimed in the revision of 1787 is to be found, in large part, in the common nouns, such as *ass* (*wild*), *discus, dove's dung, fat alley, feasts, foxes, goat* (*escape*), *ostrich, necromancer, unicorn.*

The most obvious innovation in *The Scripture Lexicon* of 1787 is the use of brackets to enclose Hebrew primitive meanings and the affixing of the Greek equivalent of the Hebrew terms, as in the following excerpts:

(1)

1784: Aaron (i.e. *a teacher, an hill; a mountain; a strong hill*) ...
1787: Aaron [Ααρων, i.e. *a teacher, an hill, a mountain, a strong hill.*]

---

[13] I have used a copy of the 1810 edition which is in the Boston Public Library.

BUK-KI'-AH, [Βαχἱϙ. Βουκίας, i. e. *the diffipation of the Lord.*] One of the muficians of the temple of *Jerufalem.*

BUL, [Βαὰλ, i. e. *changeable or perifhing.*] The eighth month of the jewifh *ecclefiaftical* or fecond month of their *civil year,* now called *Marfchevan,* anfwering to part of our *October* and *November.*

BU'-NAH, [Βαενὰ. Βενὰ, i. e. *building or underftanding.*] One of the pofterity. of the patriarch *Judah.*

BUN'-NI, [Βοννὰ, i. e. *building me.*] A Levite who returned from the babylonifh captivity.

BUZ, [Βεἕ, i. e. *defpifed or plundered.*] A nephew to the patriarch *Abraham.*

BU'-ZI, [Βεζεὶ, i. e. *my contempt.*] A jewifh prieft, the father of the prophet *Ezekiel.*

BUZ'-ITE. A defcendent of *Buz.*

C.

C *before.* A.

CAB. An *hebrew* meafure of capacity, containing about two Englifh pints.

CAB'-BON, [Χαϐϐὰν. Χαϐϱὰ, i. e. *as though underftanding.*] A city of *Palefline* in the tribe of *Judah* in the valley.

CAB'-HAM. A place of *Palefline* in the tribe of *Judah.*

CA'-BUL, [Χωϭαμασομὲλ, i. e. *difpleafing or dirty.*] The name which *Hiram,* king of *Tyre,* gave to the twenty cities given him by king *Solomon;* *Hiram* not liking them, called them *Cabul.*

CAD'-DIS.

CAD'-DIS, [Καϐϐὶς.] A name of *Joannes* the fon of *Mattathias* in the hiftory of the *Maccabees.*

CA'-DES, [Καδή;, i. e. *holinefs.*] A place in *Galilee* in *Judæa,* in the tribe of *Iffachar.*

CA'-DESH. See *Kadefh.*

CÆ'-SAR, [Καίσαϱ, i. e. *a cut or gafh.*] The general title of the *Roman* emperors.

CÆ-SAR-Æ'-A, [Καισαϱεία, i. e. *a bufh of hair.*] A place near the borders of *Philippi,* in *Macedonia* in *Afia* : now *Caifar.*

CÆ-SAR-Æ'-A PHI-LIP'-PI, [Καισαϱεία Φιλίππε.] A city of *Palefline,* fo named by *Philip* the tetrach after the *Roman* emperor and himfelf: it was called *Lefhem* and *Laifh* by the *Canaanites,* but when the children of *Dan* took it, it was called *Dan*; it was alfo called *Paneas,* from the mountain beneath which it ftood.

CA-I'-A-PHAS, [Καϊαφας, i. e. *a fearcher.*] The high prieft of the Jews at the time of our *Savior's* death.

CA'-IN, [Καἰν, i. e. *poffeffion.*] The fon of *Adam* who flew his brother *Abel*—alfo the name of a city of *Palefline,* in the tribe of *Judah,* in the mountains.

CA-I'-NAN, [Καϊνᾶν, i. e. *poffeffer, or purchafer, or one who laments.*] The fon of *Enos* the patriarch, died A. M. 1235, Æt. 910.

CAI'-RITES. A feft of Jews who adhered folely to the Scriptures.

CA'-LAH, [Χαλὰχ, i. e. *favourable, or as green fruit.*] A city of *Palefline,* in the tribe of *Afher.*

CAL'-A-MUS, [Καλάμϙ, i. e. *fweet.*] It is called *fweet cane* by the prophet *Jeremiah*—it is a fpicy root, belonging to a rufh or a flag.

CAL'-COL, [Καλχὰλ, i. e. *nourifhing ; or as confuming all things.*] A fon of *Zerah* a defcendent from the patriarch *Judah.* See *Chalcol.*

CAL'-DEES, [Χαλδαὶοι, i. e. *mingling, or as devils.*] Subjects of *Nebuchadnezzar* king of *Babylon.*

CA'-LEB, [Χάλεϐ, i. e. *a dog, crow, bafket, or the heart.*] A famous jewifh warrior, of the tribe of *Judah,*

F 2

FIG. 11. An opening from Peter Oliver's *The Scripture Lexicon* (1787).

(2)

1784: *Abaddon* (i.e. *destroying*) One of the names of the devil.

1787: *Abaddon* [Αβαδδων, i.e. *destroying*]. One of the names of the Devil, in the Hebrew tongue.

(3)

1784: *Abagtha* (i.e. *father of the wine press*) . . .

1787: *Abagtha* [Αβαγθα i.e. *father of the wine press*]

Perhaps the compiler did not need to know much Greek to supply the forms for the three words above, or, to mention a few more, for the entries of *Abana, Abarim, Abda, Abdiel, Abdon, Abednego, Abel, Abel-main*. He could, however, have found the Greek forms by consulting Brian Walton's *Biblia Sacra Polyglotta* (1657) or the Antwerp Polyglot (1572), both of which have the Biblical proper names in their indexes, together with the Hebrew and Greek equivalents in the outer margins. With his alphabetical list before him, Oliver would have found little difficulty in transferring the Greek forms to his own text. Whatever the procedure, the 1787 text continued without change into the 1797 edition[14] and in the so-called "new edition" of 1810.

For the primitive meanings of the Hebrew or Biblical proper names, the major portion of his *Lexicon*, Oliver relied almost wholly, as we have seen, on the Geneva Concordance, compiled by Robert F. Herrey. And Herrey derived much of his book from Robert Estienne's 1537 glossary and index of the Bible, entitled *Hebraea, Chaldaea, Graeca et Latina nomina*. The continuing dependence of lexicographers upon Robert Estienne's definitive work of 1537 is therefore clear in Oliver's 1787 text and in its subsequent editions even into the nineteenth century.

[14] I am indebted to Professor James Sledd who examined carefully for me copies of the 1784 and 1797 *Scripture Lexicon* in the private collection of Mr. Elsdon C. Smith, Evanston, Illinois. Professor Sledd transcribed title pages and typical entries from these two editions for comparison with entries from other editions. He also noted changes in accentuation and syllabication in the 1797 edition.

❧ VI ❧

Proper Names in
the Estienne Dictionaries

F THE *Hebraea . . . nomina,* Renouard writes with esteem. He maintains that before Estienne the multitude of Biblical proper names in Hebrew, Chaldean, Greek, and Latin had been much altered and debased in meaning by translations into the various languages and by constant reproductions of manuscripts and printed copies. Estienne restored these names to their exact original meanings, always with their Latin interpretation, and thus preserved them from future alteration. He drew from a wide range of authorities besides the Scriptures. Under *Aegyptus,* for example, he cites Pliny, Pomponius Mela, Josephus, Egesippus, Strabo, Ptolemaeus, Volaterranus, and Eusebius. Under *Babylonia* are cited Josephus, St. Augustine, Pliny, Strabo, Herodotus, Pomponius Mela, Ptolemaeus, Stephanus the Byzantine, and Volaterranus.

This extension in range of authorities, sacred and profane, in the *Hebraea . . . nomina* reflects the author's preoccupation with the subject of proper names in this period (1528–1550). In 1530 he first edited Hermann Torrentinus' *Elucidarius Carminum*; in 1536 he added proper names to his own *Dictionarium . . . Thesaurus,* and in 1543 increased their number. It seems likely that Estienne's interest in the proper-name dictionary as a genre was first aroused by the vogue and usefulness of *Elucidarius Carminum.*

In 1498 Torrentinus, a classical scholar and teacher of rhetoric at the College of Groningen, first published his *Elucidarius.* His purpose was to answer concisely inquiries which he had received repeatedly from his students and other readers concerning the meanings of proper names and their allusions in Latin and Greek literature. As a convenience to his readers and an economy for himself he compiled and published the helpful handbook which he called *Elucidarius Carminum et historiarum, vel Vocabularius* ("the elucidator or explicator of poems and histories").[1] This book soon gained wide popularity, and was printed repeatedly at various cities on the Continent. By the time of Torrentinus' death in 1520, the *Elucidarius* had gone through at least eleven printings.[2] A few examples from the 1514 text will give an idea of the content. The items may be translated thus:

Apelles, a most excellent painter from the Island of Co [Cous] or from Ephesus, who on his death left an unfinished portrait of Venus, which no one has dared to complete.

Atlas was king of Mauritania, who is said to have invented the study of astronomy. It is also a high mountain in Mauritania, which the neighboring people called the pillar of the sky. The poets feign that Atlas was a great giant who held up the firmament.

Cacus was a robber in Italy, who burned whole villas; wherefore he was called the son of Vulcan. Finally, he was killed by Hercules, whose cattle he had stolen. Verg. Some suppose he was the servant of King Evander.

Daphne, daughter of the river Peneus, in Thessaly. When Apollo loved her and pursued her, she is said to have been turned into a laurel tree. Ouid. primo *Metamor.*

---

[1] The University of Texas Humanities Research Center has three copies of the *Elucidarius*: (1) Hagenau, 1514; (2) Antwerp, 1545, augmented by Robert Estienne; (3) Venice, 1548, without augmentation.

For an essay on Torrentinus and his *Elucidarius,* see D. T. Starnes, "The Poetic Dictionary and the Poet," *The Library Chronicle* (The University of Texas), II (1946), 75–85. See also entry on H. Torrentinus in *Allgemeine Deutsche Biographie,* II, 245; Michaud's *Biographie Universelle Ancienne et Moderne* (nouvelle édition, Paris, n.d.).

[2] Editions are recorded as follows: Deventer, 1498, 1501, 1513; Argentinae [Strasbourg], 1505, 1514, 1518; Hagenau, 1507, 1510, 1512, 1514; Lare, 1515. See *Catalogue Général des Livres Imprimés de la Bibliothèque Nationale* (Paris, 1912). Compare also the *British Museum Catalogue.*

Renouard (I, 34) estimates more than fifteen printings of the *Elucidarius* before 1530.

Pathmos, a small island in the Aegean sea, one of the Cyclades in which the divine John the evangelist, in exile, wrote the Apocalypse.

Scythia, a large and barbarous country in the north extending from India to Germany. It has the sea on one side and the Riphean mountains on the other.

From the examples given, it is easy to see the range and usefulness of the *Elucidarius* to students of classical literature at the beginning of the sixteenth century. Largely through the efforts of Robert Estienne its value was to be enhanced and its influence extended for another century and a half. In the sketch of Torrentinus in *Allgemeine Deutsche Biographie* we read: "Elucidarius . . . welches zuerst 1498 zu Deventer erschien und der erste Versuch auf diesem Gebiete war"; and in *Biographie Universelle*, "Cet opuscule est le premier essai que l'on connaisse d'un dictionnaire historique contenant aussi la mythologie et la géographie ancienne."

Robert Estienne was quick to recognize the value of the *Elucidarius Carminum*. He had prepared his glossary for the *Biblia* of 1528 and was to augment it for the 1532 edition. Just as this glossary was, in fact, a proper-name dictionary for the Scriptures, so should there be, he must have thought, a similar work for the classics, or profane literature. Useful though the *Elucidarius* was, Robert Estienne knew it was really inadequate, and, using this text as a basis, he set about correcting and expanding it. His first revision of the *Elucidarius* was published in 1530; the title page read: *"Dictionarium poeticum, quod vulgo inscribatur Elucidarius Carminum . . .* ex officina Roberti Stephani: Parisiis, M.D.XXX." Under Estienne's editorship the *Elucidarius* continued to be published for almost twenty years,[3] with occasional variations of title, as in that of 1541—*Dictionarius propriorum nominum*.

Estienne's Antwerp edition of 1545 reinstates the term *Elucidarius*, and the phrasing of the title page is a close parallel (contrasting only in aim) to that of the *Hebraea . . . nomina*. Compare the titles:

[3] Editions in 1530, 1535, 1541, 1545, 1550, 1554, 1559.
  Cf. Renouard, I, 253; see also *Catalogue Général* and the *British Museum Catalogue*.

1545: *Elucidarius poeticus, siue Dictionarium nominum propriorum viro-*
 rum, mulierum, populorum, idolorum, urbium, fluuiorum, montium, caeterorumque locorum quae passim in libris prophanis
 leguntur.[4]

1537: *Hebraea, Chaldaea, Graeca et Latina nomina virorum,* mulierum,
 populorum, idolorum, vrbium, montium, caeterorumque locorum,
 quae in Bibliis leguntur, restituta, cum Latina interpretatione.

Obviously, at that time Robert Estienne had in mind companion
volumes: one treating sacred or Scriptural names, the other, profane or
classical names. Not until his 1553 *Dictionarium historicum* did he
combine all the entries in a single alphabet and a single folio volume.

Of the 1541 revision of the *Elucidarius,* Mrs. Armstrong writes that
Estienne "recognized there the services rendered by the *Elucidarius
Carminum* or *Dictionarium Poeticum* (which he himself had reprinted), but his compilation deals more completely and systematically
with the proper names found in ancient literature."[5] These words are
applicable also to the 1545 Antwerp edition, in which *Elucidarius* is
again part of the title. On the verso of the title page of this edition
Estienne states that he is offering the reader a dictionary of proper
names—a work that is new, never before published. He maintains that
Torrentinus' little book, commonly called *Elucidarius Carminum,* did
not contain a good part of the proper names, and such as it did have—
feigned, rude, and disordered—could not be very profitable to students. But Estienne has collected fables from Servius and Acron, has
borrowed from grammarians, and from celebrated writers has collected
the histories of renowned men, illustrating their lives by their deeds
and sayings. For whatever pertains to the names of places, the sites of
cities, and the sizes of rivers he has carefully studied original classical
authorities, so that the accounts seem not so much written by him as
dictated by the authors themselves—Pliny, Strabo, Ptolemy.

Estienne's claims for the 1545 *Elucidarius poeticus* are amply sup-
ported. This thick octavo volume goes far beyond the *Elucidarius* of
Torrentinus (which, incidentally, continued to be published, without

---

[4] The 1545 title from a copy in The University of Texas Humanities Research Center; the 1537 title from my own copy.

[5] Armstrong, *Robert Estienne,* p. 90.

amplification, in the original author's name, as in an edition at Venice, 1548). Estienne's volume corrects and expands entries found in the original and adds thousands of new entries. With this 1545 edition, the Estienne text became a fairly ample dictionary of classical proper names, including those of places, of men, both historical and legendary, of myths and gods and goddesses. The proper-name entries distributed through the text of the 1536 *Dictionarium . . . Thesaurus* and augmented in the 1543 edition are of almost contemporary composition.

All the industry involved in compiling these volumes was a logical preparation for a single volume which would embrace Biblical and classical (sacred and profane) names. To achieve such a work, no one was better prepared than Robert Estienne. After 1545 he had at his disposal the alphabetized list of Biblical names in the *Hebraea . . . nomina* and the classical names in the revised *Elucidarius poeticus* and in the *Dictionarium . . . Thesaurus,* all with the pertinent descriptions and explanations. With these lists before him, what could have been easier than to combine them into one and thus produce a single volume containing the substance of all three? In this task Robert Estienne may have been engaged before he felt it necessary to leave Paris in 1550.

It is important here to remember the disturbed religious conditions throughout the stormy career of Robert Estienne. His determination, from 1523 on, in printing the Scriptures in whole or in part, to publish correct texts, and to make the Bible known to all brought continuous bitter and unjust attacks upon him until, with the death of his friend and protector, Francis I, he was forced to flee to Geneva for protection. There he set up his press and continued printing until his death in 1559.

Meantime, Charles Estienne, versed in classical literature and trained in the art of printing like his brother Robert, assumed charge of the family printing office in 1551 and was made guardian of Robert's children.[6] According to Larousse, Charles remained faithful to the Catholic religion, guarded the interests of his nephews, and finished printing the books begun by Robert.[7]

Charles Estienne began to take over Robert's press in the latter part

---

[6] See Armstrong, *Robert Estienne,* p. 224, and McMurtrie, *The Book,* p. 331.
[7] Pierre Larousse, *La Grande Encyclopédie,* VII, 976.

of 1551, according to Mrs. Armstrong, printing Brunellus, *Epistolae* (September 19), Clenardus, *Institutiones linguae graecae* (October 7), and Cicero, *Paradoxa* (December 20). All these editions, like the Appian, bore the statement "Cura ac diligentia Caroli Stephani"—a formula which means the printing was done on behalf of someone else. If a sixteenth-century printer was the actual publisher of a book and used the formula "Cura ac diligentia," he added to it "et sumptibus" or "impensis." Mrs. Armstrong says that "Dr. Estienne's expression is on the whole that of a man printing on behalf of some one else, supplying only the work and skill."[8] It is obvious that the four books listed above were printed for Robert Estienne, the real editor. The policy of the Estienne family, however, after the departure of Robert, was to transfer the more important works to the name of Charles. "Dans les circonstances difficiles," writes Brandon, "où la famille se trouvait, on aura cru agir pour le mieux en transférant au nom de Charles les fonds les plus importantes de l'imprimerie."[9]

In 1552, for example, Charles printed *Dictionarium Latino-Gallicum* with the credit "Parisiis, apud Carolum Stephanum typographum Regium." Authorship of this book has sometimes been ascribed to Charles, but we know that it was compiled by Robert and that editions had appeared in 1538 and 1546. Very similar was the case of *Dictionariolum puerorum*. This small dictionary was compiled and published by Robert Estienne, first in 1544 and again in 1547. It was reprinted by Charles in 1552, and, like the *Dictionarium Latino-Gallicum,* it bore his name—another example of family policy. This attitude of the Estienne family helps explain a 1553 publication to be discussed now.

The work I refer to has this wording on the title page:

Dictionarium historicum ac Poeticum: Omnia Gentium, hominum, locorum, fluminum ac montium antique recentioraque ad sacras ac prophanas historias poetarumque fabulas intelligendas necessaria vocabula, bono ordine complectens.

[Here is a woodcut of the Estienne printer's device of the olive tree, with some broken branches.]

---

[8] Armstrong, *Robert Estienne,* p. 224; cf. Renouard, *Annales,* I, 102.

[9] Edgar Ewing Brandon, *Robert Estienne et le dictionnaire français,* p. 122.

Lutetiae
Cura ac diligentia Caroli Stephani
M.D.LIII
Cum Privilegio Regis.[10]

In the phrase "ad sacras ac prophanas," etc., of this title, the editor explains that this 1553 *Dictionarium historicum* comprehends in good order (that is, in one alphabet) all words necessary to the understanding of sacred and profane histories (writings) and the fables of poets.

It is obvious that it combines the ideas and echoes the language of the two companion volumes compiled and published by Robert: *Hebraea . . . nomina* (1537) and *Elucidarius poeticus* (1545).

Looking again at the title page quoted above, one notes that special prominence is given to the printer's formula, "Cura ac diligentia Caroli Stephani," which does not mean that Charles was the compiler or author of the 1553 text. The formula means that Charles, the printer, saw this book through the press (for his brother Robert, then in Geneva) as he had done in 1551 with four other texts which bore the same formula. Charles made no claim to authorship. Nor did the address to the reader from the printer, Carolus Stephanus, seek to establish a claim of authorship for the printer. He refers to this book as a historical index of all the (Estienne) dictionaries which had appeared thus far, and the most ample. Its aim, he says, is to facilitate quick understanding not only of the proper names in Hebrew, Greek, and Latin authors, but also of historical episodes, the figments and fables of ancient poets, the deeds of heroes, the location of regions and places, and the descriptions of mountains and rivers. The aim and content of this more ample book comprehend those found in Robert's *Hebraea . . . nomina* and the enlarged *Elucidarius poeticus,* with amplifications from other sources.

After thus describing the content and purpose of the book, Charles writes these words:

Quem a fratre [Robert] iampridem inchoatum laborem, atque a nobis nunc demum quam diligentissime fieri potuit dispositum, ac multum locupletatum . . .

[10] This title page is transcribed from a microfilm copy of the 1553 *Dictionarium historicum* in the University of Michigan Library. All references in this study are to this edition.

This statement is somewhat vague and lacking in specific information. Yet we learn that this work was begun some time ago by his brother, who can be none other than Robert, though his name, as a matter of policy, is not specifically mentioned. The *Dictionarium historicum ac poeticum* was, then, another work by Robert, not yet ready for the press when he had to leave Paris. Now, at length, Charles continues, the matter has been arranged or ordered (that is, put in alphabetical order as carefully as possible ("quam diligentissime fieri potuit") and, to continue with Charles' phrasing ("ac multum locupletatum"), much amplified or enriched. By whom? Presumably, by Charles himself. The claim is a more or less conventional one even when augmentation is minimal and seems to be impossible to confirm. Analysis of the content of the 1553 *Dictionarium historicum* will show that the amplifications are, in any event, from Robert's own books and from books which he had used for reference works elsewhere.

The last sentence in Charles' address to the reader may be paraphrased thus:

We promise you, in good faith, there is nothing here which could in any way undermine the Christian religion (about which we well know there is to be no levity) nor the authority of the prince, nor the prestige of the Doctors [of Theology].

This expression indicates, as does the whole address, cautious procedure in transferring to Charles the responsibility for the printing of Robert's work.

Even this prudent behavior was apparently not very successful. The *Dictionarium historicum* thus set forth and published in 1553 was not again printed for eight years. Was it because it was known to be essentially Robert's work and because he was in bad repute with the authorities?

In 1561 another edition of this extensive proper-name dictionary was published in Paris. The wording of the title, *Dictionarium historicum ac poeticum . . .,* corresponds verbatim to that in the 1553 text. Then these words are added:

A Carolo Stephano, illius authore, postremo hoc labore multum adauctum, vt ex notis singulis accessionum adscriptis facile conspicies.

[Here is a woodcut of the printer's device]

Lutetiae. Apud Ioannem Macaeum, sub Scuto Britanniae, monte D. Hylarij. 1561. Cum priuilegio Regis.[11]

On the verso of the title page is printed the "Priuilège du Roy," granted by King Charles to Iehan Macé to have the exclusive right to print and sell, for a period of six years, a book entitled *Dictionarium Poeticum & historicum propriorum nominum fluuiorum, montium . . .* The wording of the title in the "Priuilège" varies slightly from that on the title page, echoing the phrasing of the 1545 *Elucidarius poeticus.* The Latin address to the reader is largely a revamping of a similar address in the 1553 edition. Though ascribed to Carolus Stephanus, this 1561 address may be by Iehan Macé, the printer.

Words quoted above, "A Carolo Stephano, illius authore . . ." from the title page of the 1561 text, are ambiguous. Although they imply that Charles was the author of the 1561 edition, as of the 1553, they say only that he augmented the 1561.[12] The "Priuilège" indicates that the book was revised, corrected, and amplified by "Maistre Charles Estienne," Doctor of Medicine, and other learned men. The language of the title page and the Royal Privilege of 1561, when analyzed, means that Charles Estienne and others made some augmentation of the book. There is no case for Charles' authorship, and it is significant that Iehan Macé, not Charles Estienne, had the King's Privilege and the exclusive right to print and sell this *Dictionarium historicum* for six years.

In the early months of 1561 Charles Estienne was still printing in Paris.[13] For example, in February he printed an augmented edition of the *Dictionarium Latino-Gallicum,* of which Robert was the original author. If Charles were the author of the 1553 and 1561 texts, why did Macé have complete control of the printing and selling of this book at this time? Why, also, did Macé insist upon starring the new entries in the 1561 edition? It seems not unlikely that doubt had been expressed as to Charles' contribution to the earlier edition and that starred entries and his name on the title page, though the language was

[11] I have used a copy of this edition in the Humanities Research Center of The University of Texas.

[12] The 1553 edition contains 612 pages; 1561 has 650 pages, or about 40 pages more.

[13] See Renouard, *Annales,* I, 112–113.

ambiguous, were intended, probably without his consent, to support the authorship of Charles.

Commenting on the 1553 *Dictionarium historicum*, Renouard states that this book was printed again in 1566, at Geneva, two years after Charles' death.[14] It would seem that Renouard had not seen the 1561 edition, printed at Paris by Macé, but only the first of the two editions published in Charles' lifetime. In this first edition Charles refrained, as we have seen, from claiming authorship; nevertheless, Renouard remarks that Charles has always been identified as the original author (". . . toujours reconnu comme ayant Charles Estienne pour auteur primitif").[15] Assertion is not evidence, however. Renouard does not say who has made such an identification nor on what grounds. He does not make a comparative study of the texts involved to show how much Charles contributed and what relationship the 1553 edition bore to the lexical labors of Robert.

We should remember that for almost thirty years before he left his printing establishment in Paris in 1550, Robert Estienne devoted much time to compiling and publishing dictionaries, with proper names and proper-name lexicons receiving some special attention. He had doubtless collected a vast amount of material. Charles, like his brother a competent classical scholar, devoted his time, however, to compiling books on agriculture—gardens, meadows, vineyards, trees, etc.—and on medicine, and architecture. He compiled and published in 1536 a collection of Latin and Greek names of trees, fruits, and birds (*De latinis et graecis nominibus arborum fruticum avium*).[16] He was not, however, a lexicographer who had spent years collecting and explaining proper names.[17] In printing the *Dictionarium historicum* of 1553, he was using the matter collected and published by Robert, the experienced lexicographer, and the 1561 edition published by Iehan Macé, but by inference ascribed to Charles, took over the same material and added only a relatively small percentage of new terms. The core of the materials in both the 1553 and 1561 editions was the work of Robert Estienne.

Analysis of the 1553 *Dictionarium historicum ac poeticum* reveals

---

[14] *Ibid.,* II, 260.   [15] *Ibid.*   [16] *Ibid.,* 352 ff.
[17] Charles' *Dictionarium Latino-Graecum,* 1554, was excerpted largely from Budaeus, as the title page states.

these books as principal sources of the matter: (1) Robert Estienne's own *Hebraea . . . nomina* (1537); (2) his *Elucidarius poeticus* (1545); and (3) his *Dictionarium . . . Thesaurus* (1543); (4) the *De Urbibus* of Stephanus the Byzantine (1521); and (5) the *Ecclesiasticae Historiae* lib. x, of Eusebius (printed by Robert Estienne, 1544).[18] Perhaps one should add, as minor sources, Flavius Blondus, the fifteenth-century historian whose work is cited frequently in the 1553 *Dictionarium historicum*; and Polydore Vergil, *History of England.*

The first step in making the *Dictionarium historicum*, which was ultimately published in 1553, was the combining of the *Hebraea . . . nomina* and the *Elucidarius poeticus* to produce a proper-name dictionary containing the names in the Scriptures and those in ancient classical literature. This appears to have been done by Robert before he left Paris, and these volumes constituted the core of the new text. One must infer from Charles' (the printer's) 1553 address to the reader that the combination was already made before he entered the project.

One test of the relationship of the *Hebraea . . . nomina* to the *Dictionarium historicum* is to compare the first 50 entries under each of the randomly chosen letters *B, D, L, M* in the two books.

B (*Baal* to *Banaa*): All except 2 of the first 50 entries are incorporated, sometimes successively, sometimes with intervals, in the *Dictionarium historicum.*

D (*Dabai* to *Diana*): All except 4 are incorporated.

L (*Laabim* to *Linus*): All except 4 are incorporated.

M (*Maacha* to *Magog*): All except 2 are incorporated.

Stating the results concisely, we find that of the 200 entries examined in *Hebraea . . . nomina*, all but 12 are incorporated in the *Dictionarium historicum.*

There is one modification which the compiler of the *Dictionarium historicum* makes: he omits the Latin phrases for the primitive Hebrew meaning. Here is an example:

Hebraea . . . nomina

Baalim, Idola, siue dominantes, aut subiecientes vel possidentes. Nomen idoli, 1. reg. a. 2 paral. 18. a. iere.

18 Renouard, *Annales,* I, 59.

Dictionarium historicum

Baalim, nomen idoli, 1. reg. 7. a. 2 paral. 18. a. iere.[19]

A similar comparison may be made of the first 50 entries in the *Elucidarius poeticus,* as revised and augmented for the *Dictionarium historicum.*

A (*Aba* to *Abudiacum*): All the first 50 entries are incorporated in the *Dictionarium historicum.*

B (*Baba* to *Barbarium*): All first 50 are incorporated.

C (*Cabalaca* to *Cainas*): All first 50 except *Caelesttina* are incorporated.

M (*Macae* to *Manius Marcus*): All first 50 are incorporated.

Further, the first 50 entries under *L* are incorporated in the *Dictionarium historicum,* as are all 80 entries under *R* and all 25 entries under *Z.* Sometimes the incorporations have been taken in clusters or in successive entries from earlier texts, as in the first 16 names under the letter *B,* all of which derive originally from *Hebraea . . . nomina.* More frequently the borrowed words and descriptions from the earlier dictionaries are separated by matter from other sources. In the *Dictionarium historicum* there is also some rearrangement to improve alphabetical order, and occasional modifications. For example, in the case of *Aegyptus,* with different descriptive details from the two sources, the compiler of 1553 takes both, making separate entries. But he combines *Africa* and *Aphrica,* from the original texts, in a single entry. In *Arabia,* somewhat expanded, most of the matter is from the 1545 *Elucidarius poeticus,* though there are details from *Hebraea . . . nomina.* These examples indicate that the borrowing was not uncritical, though the 1553 *Dictionarium historicum* absorbed both of Robert's earlier texts for almost 60 per cent of its content.

Another approach affords information which is more comprehensive and reveals that the debt to Robert Estienne is even greater. In the 1553 text there are approximately 800 entries under the letter *I* (*I* and *J* are put together as one letter in these early texts). Of these entries, 323 derive from *Hebraea . . . nomina* and 161 from *Elucidarius poeti-*

---

[19] In later editions of the *Dictionarium historicum* the omissions are restored and the entry given in full according to the original.

cus; these two texts account for a little more than 50 per cent of *Dictionarium historicum* entries. This is not all. There are, for example, some 57 references to Stephanus the Byzantine. These take the form of "Steph.," "Stephano," or "Stephanus." The references are to his *De Urbibus*, first published (in Greek) in Venice in 1502 and then in Florence in 1521.[20] This work is cited frequently by Robert Estienne in his *Dictionarium . . . Thesaurus,* and the revisions of the *Dictionarium historicum* used *De Urbibus* extensively for names of cities, towns, and villages.

What we may regard as the new element in the 1553 text is the introduction of the names of historical personages—kings, popes, princes, pontifexes, consuls, etc. These entries are as a rule very concise, giving only the name, rank, and time of the character—little more, in fact, than identification. For these, the revisers frequently cite Eusebius' *Ecclesiastical Histories* and the *Chronicle* (they cite the Latin forms), as in the entries *Johannes Apostolus, Johannes Chrysostom,* and *Innocentius Falsus.* In such entries Eusebius is often the source of information even when not referred to. Under the letter *I* there are 106 entries which seem to derive from Eusebius. It is worth special note that Robert Estienne printed *Eusebii Pamphili Ecclesiasticae* lib. x in Paris in 1544, and also *Evangelicae Preparationis* lib. xv, etc.[21] The Eusebius was thus familiar and easily accessible to him and his assistants.

Analyzing Robert Estienne's total contribution to the 1553 *Dictionarium historicum,* we find, under *R* for example, that his work would account for about 90 per cent of the content of the entries.[22]

Ascription to Charles Estienne (Carolus Stephanus) of the authorship of the 1553 *Dictionarium historicum* and the uncritical acceptance of this ascription by succeeding generations of printers and publishers

[20] Brunet, *Manuel du Libraire,* IV, 257–258.

[21] Renouard, *Annales,* I, 59.

[22] If we disregard 17 cross references as duplicates, we have in the 1553 edition a total of 304 entries. Of these, 103 derive from Robert's *Hebraea . . . nomina* and 80 from his *Elucidarius poeticus.* From these two texts the 1553 edition draws 60 per cent of its entries. If we add to these results the 44 entries from Eusebius and 45 from Stephanus the Byzantine, as the responsibility of Robert, then his work would account for about 90 per cent of the *R* entries.

is without foundation in fact. The evidence, external and internal, points to Robert Estienne as the real author.

There is no indication that the *Dictionarium historicum* had a wide vogue during I. Macé's control of the printing and sale, as granted by the Royal Privilege, from about 1560 to 1565. But at expiration of the "Priuilège" an edition was printed by J. Perrinus at Geneva, 1566, and from this period on, the book enjoyed wide popularity, there being at least seven editions between 1566 and 1596 and also eleven editions between 1608 and 1693.[23] When Robert Estienne died in 1559 his eldest son, Henri II, took over the press at Geneva. Though the Estienne *Dictionarium historicum* was printed at Geneva, Lyons, and various other cities on the Continent from 1566 on, it was never printed by the Estienne press after 1553.

From the beginning the *Elucidarius poeticus* and its revisions by Robert Estienne contained historical-biographical sketches of the ancients, but the emphasis was at first on the poetic or mythological element. In its expanded 1553 form the historical matter received greater attention and was extended to include many later historical characters, both secular and religious; the title was also changed to include the word *historicum: Dictionarium historicum ac poeticum.* By 1590 the title was to give prominence to another feature, which, in fact, had been present from the beginning—the geographic. The title then read *Dictionarium historicum, geographicum, poeticum,* and this title it was to retain through many editions, almost to the end of the seventeenth century. From 1567 on there were augmentations by anonymous editors, including additional matter from Robert Estienne's own *Hebraea . . . nomina* and *Dictionarium . . . Thesaurus,* from Comes' *Mythologia* and Cartari's *Imagines Deorum* for the mythology, and from Ortelius and other geographers.

The wide vogue of the Estienne *Dictionarium historicum* was evidenced not only by the large number of editions published from the 1560's on but also by the fact that this book, along with Robert's

---

[23] Dates of sixteenth-century editions printed at Paris, Lyons, Geneva, and elsewhere on the Continent were 1566, 1567, 1575, 1579, 1581, 1591, 1595.

Compare *Catalogue Général des Livres Imprimés de la Bibliothèque Nationale* (Paris, 1912) and the *British Museum Catalogue.*

Dictionarium . . . Thesaurus and (after 1565) Cooper's *Thesaurus* were a part of the standard equipment of school libraries and individual libraries. As Professor Ernest William Talbert has pointed out,[24] there were copies in the individual libraries of Queen Mary; John Palsgrave (that famous tutor of princesses and dukes); King James I; Robert Burton; Richard Stonely (Elizabeth's embezzling teller); and Elizabeth herself. Copies appeared in the school libraries of the Merchant Taylors' School, the library of St. Albans, and the Stratford grammar school. Thus proper names as listed and described in the Estienne dictionaries were well known to Elizabethan schoolmasters and schoolboys and to their successors in the seventeenth century. Latin-English lexicographers borrowed freely from their French antecedents, and contemporary English writers showed familiarity with the myths and legends thus transmitted.

[24] DeWitt T. Starnes and Ernest W. Talbert, *Classical Myth and Legend in Renaissance Dictionaries*, pp. 111 ff.

❧ VII ❦

The Impact of Estienne's Dictionaries in England

HE ACCOUNT of Estienne's activities thus far has indicated unity of purpose and method in his labors as editor and glossator of the *Biblia* and in his making of proper-name dictionaries. With the aim of rendering the Scriptures more intelligible to the reader, he compiled a glossary of proper names and a comprehensive index of the Old and New Testaments; these were published together in 1537 in a small volume entitled *Hebraea . . . nomina*—a book of considerable influence on the multilingual polyglot glossaries and indexes and especially on the Concordance of the Geneva Bible. Parallel with his lexical effort in editing the *Biblia* was his development of the *Elucidarius Carminum* of Torrentinus, a dictionary of proper classical names and companion volume to his glossary of Scriptural names, the *Hebraea . . . nomina*. These, together with matter from other sources, were combined to make the *Dictionarium historicum ac poeticum,* first published in 1553, of great usefulness to readers and authors of the Renaissance.[1]

In his own day, however, Estienne was even better known for his more comprehensive dictionaries: *Dictionarium . . . Thesaurus,* concerned with the whole range of Latin language and usage; and *Dictionarium Latino-Gallicum,* concerned with the Latin and French languages, exclusive of proper names. To these may be added, as of minor importance, the small school dictionaries: *Dictionnaire françois-latin* and *Dictionariolum puerorum.* This chapter is devoted to the study of

---

[1] Suggestions and illustrations for this chapter may be found widely dispersed through a dozen chapters in my *Renaissance Dictionaries.*

the impact of these dictionaries on bilingual lexicographers in England, and to a survey of their influence on English literature.

As early as 1545 the influence of Robert Estienne on lexicography in England was manifest. In that year Sir Thomas Elyot published a revised edition of his Latin-English dictionary with the title *Bibliotheca Eliotae*. Elyot's dictionary of 1538 had been criticized for depending too much on Friar Calepine's *Dictionarium*. In the 1545 *Bibliotheca* Elyot dropped his earlier pilot and silently chose another. The augmentation of the latter volume, investigation shows, depended upon Robert Estienne's *Dictionarium Latino-Gallicum* (1538). Expansion of the earlier entries and definitions and introduction of new entries and new illustrations came directly from Robert Estienne's dictionary. A comparison of entries in the two texts, under *Confero* and under *Persequor,* will suggest the close relationship.

Bibliotheca Eliotae (1545)	*Dictionarium Latino-Gallicum* (1538)
Conficere pensum, to spyn out her threde.	*Pensum conficere,* Acheuer sa fusee.
Conficere prandium, to haue dined.	*Prandium conficere,* Acheuer le disner.
Conficere solicitudines alicui, to bryng one into heuyness or to make hym sorrowfull.	*Solicitudines alicui conficere,* Le mettre en soulci.
Persequi ius suum, to defende his ryght.	*Persequi ius suum,* Defendre & poursuyvre son droict.
Persequi poenas alicuius, to reuenge ones deathe.	*Persequi poenas alicuius,* Venger la mort d'aucun.
Persequi promissa alicuius, to solicite one to kepe his promyse.	*Persequi promissa alterius,* Soliciter qu'il tienne sa promesse.
Persequi vita disciplinam recte vivendi, to lyue accordynge to the doctrine of lyuynge honestly.	*Persequi vita disciplinam recte vivendi,* Viure selon la discipline de bien viure.

After Elyot's death in 1546 the Reverend Thomas Cooper, classical scholar and schoolmaster, took over the editorship of the *Bibliotheca*. In 1548 he published another edition of this book, augmented, he assures the reader, by 33,000 words. Although it is not clear what

Cooper meant by "33,000 words," whether terms to be defined or merely definitions and illustrations of usage, it is obvious that he made a considerable augmentation and that the source of this expansion was again the *Dictionarium Latino-Gallicum* of Robert Estienne. Cooper's revision of the *Bibliotheca* was much more extensive than was that of Elyot. Cooper rearranged the entries to correspond to those in Estienne's Latin-French text and also translated the French definitions and illustrations into English. Compare, for example, the following entries from Cooper's edition of the *Bibliotheca* (1548) and Estienne's *Dictionarium Latino-Gallicum* (1538).

Bibliotheca Eliotae (1548)	*Dictionarium Latino-Gallicum* (1538)
Conferre omnia sua in aliquem, to do all the pleasures that one can for a man.	*Conferre sua omnia studia in aliquem,* Luy faire tous plaisirs & seruices . . . .
Benignitatem in aliquem conferre, to shewe great liberalitie or gentilnesse to one, to dooe many pleasures for him.	*Conferre benignitatem in aliquem,* Accumuler beaucoup de plaisirs enuers aucun . . .
Castra castris conferri, to pitche or campe ouer ryght agaynst another.	*Castra castris conferri,* Rapporter son camp au camp des ennemys; & mettre vis a vis.
Coram inter nos conferemus, we wyll deuys and common of these matters, whan we meet together.	*Coram inter nos conferemus,* Nous en parlerons & diuiserons ensemble.
Maledicta in aliquem conferre, to rayle or geue one shrewde wordes.	*Conferre maledicta in aliquem,* Dire beaucoup d'oultrages a aucun.
Ingenium ad rem aliquam, to geue ones minde to a thynge.	*Ingenium ad rem aliquam conferre,* Employer son esprit a quelque chose.
Conficere ambulationem, to walke.	*Conficere ambulationem pomeridianam in aliquo loco,* S'y pourmener.
Absolutionem conficere, to dispache or quitte.	*Absolutionem conficere,* Expedier.

In the 1548 *Bibliotheca,* then, as revised by Cooper, were the rearranged entries which Elyot originally borrowed from Estienne, and thousands of Cooper's definitions and illustrations which depended upon Estienne's *Dictionarium Latino-Gallicum* (1538). Though Cooper claimed additional expansion of the 1552 and 1559 editions of the *Bibliotheca,* assertion of a further debt to Estienne is hardly safe. Cooper does not refer, in these issues or in the earlier one of 1548, to the debt to Estienne.

Estienne's *Dictionarium Latino-Gallicum* and Cooper's *Thesaurus*

In 1565 Thomas Cooper first published his *Thesaurus linguae Romanae et Britannicae* and became a lexicographer in his own right. This book speedily became the standard authority among Latin-English dictionaries and was reissued in 1573, 1584, and 1587, with but slight augmentations. Cooper's *Thesaurus* absorbed the *Bibliotheca Eliotae* and borrowed freely from other sources, especially from Robert Estienne. Cooper intimated, in his address to the reader, that he was indebted to Estienne's *Dictionarium, seu linguae Latinae Thesaurus.* This book was first published in 1531, in folio. Another folio edition appeared in 1536 in two volumes and, in 1543, another folio edition in three volumes. Cooper undoubtedly knew this *Dictionarium . . . Thesaurus* since it was a basic work for other dictionaries by the French author, but Cooper's debt to this book was indirect.

A comparative study shows, instead, beyond a doubt, that Estienne's later *Dictionarium Latino-Gallicum* (1552, 1561) was the major source of Cooper's *Thesaurus.* The word lists and definitions, the illustrations and arrangements on the pages are too similar to be accidental. Cooper, of course, drew from other sources, such as his occasional borrowings from Frisius' Latin-German dictionary (itself based on Estienne's *Dictionarium . . . Thesaurus*), but the principal source was the Latin-French text of Estienne.

Evidence supporting this conclusion may be found in a detailed comparison of definitions and illustrations of almost any group of entries, for example, the matter under *Confero* and *Conficio.* Tracing and comparing these in the various texts concerned, as in Estienne's *Dictionarium . . . Thesaurus* and his *Dictionarium Latino-Gallicum,* Frisius' *Dictionarium Latino-Germanicum,* the *Bibliotheca Eliotae* (1548), and Cooper's *Thesaurus* (1565), will make clear the interrelationships:

1) The rather ample general definition of a term in Cooper's *Thesaurus* comes from the revised *Bibliotheca Eliotae*.

2) Cooper has a number of English equivalents of Latin phrases for which there is no corresponding source in Estienne's *Dictionarium Latino-Gallicum* or in Frisius.

3) In each entry in which the texts show corresponding vernacular interpretations, Cooper's *Thesaurus* derives, in most instances, from Estienne.

4) Frisius' *Dictionarium,* based on Estienne, is sometimes the source of Cooper's definition or illustration.[2]

An hour or so of study of Cooper's *Thesaurus* with Estienne's *Dictionarium Latino-Gallicum* open beside it will reveal the dependence of Cooper on his French source.

Major borrowings from Cooper's *Thesaurus* are found in the *Dictionarium* of Thomas Thomas (1587), in John Rider's *Bibliotheca Scholastica* (1589), in the Rider-Holyoke dictionaries (1604–1657), in works by Francis Gouldman (1664) and Adam Littleton (1678), and on to the end of the seventeenth century. All of these lexicographers were directly or indirectly indebted to Cooper, and, through him, to Estienne.

But this is not all. When Robert Ainsworth published his *Thesaurus, or Compendious Dictionary* in 1728 he not only used materials from his immediate predecessors already indebted to Estienne, but for his method—arrangement of definitions and illustrations of them—he returned to the great Latin *Dictionarium . . . Thesaurus* of Robert Estienne as a model of organization and, in part, a source of information.

Estienne's Schoolboy Dictionaries in England

In 1552 Jean Veron, a French citizen resident in England, published his *Dictionariolum puerorum, tribus linguis, Latina, Anglica, et Gallica conscriptum*. According to Rudolph Waddington, who published a much revised and altered edition of Veron's book in 1572, Veron's text of 1552 was based upon Robert Estienne's *Dictionariolum puerorum*. Veron merely added English to Estienne's little book for schoolboys. The English phrases and sentences are inserted between the Latin

[2] See Starnes, *Renaissance Dictionaries,* pp. 91–93.

and French of the Estienne text, thus making a little dictionary in three languages, the English being Veron's translation of the French.

The *Dictionariolum* of Robert Estienne was first published in Paris in 1542 and reissued in 1544 and 1547. A second edition appeared in 1550 (reprinted in 1552) and a third edition in 1557.[3] Comparison of a series of entries, for example, *Condemno, Condenso, Condico, Confectus, Confessus,* in the Veron and Estienne texts shows clearly that the English insertions by Veron are rather literal translations of Estienne's French.

After twenty-odd years the Veron dictionary was revised and much augmented as to Latin and English phrases, and the French phrases were dropped. The first revision was by Rudolph Waddington in 1575. Many of his additions were from the Elyot-Cooper Latin-English dictionaries. The final revision was in 1584 by Abraham Fleming, who made some additions to the illustrative phrases, drawing his materials from Cooper's *Thesaurus.*

In the process of revision by Waddington and then by Fleming the English phrases of Veron were fused with the English from the Elyot-Cooper dictionaries. As Elyot and Cooper had also borrowed freely from Estienne's Latin-French dictionaries, as had Veron, the two revisions of the Veron dictionary were saturated with matter directly or indirectly from Robert Estienne's dictionaries.

Estienne's French-Latin Texts
and the Huloet Dictionaries

In 1552, the year in which Jean Veron published his version of the *Dictionariolum,* Richard Huloet printed his *Abcedarium Anglico Latinum,* an English-Latin dictionary for beginners (*pro Tyrunculis*). In the preliminary matter Huloet speaks of his book as "a paterne or prothotipe newly inuented." He refers to his method of presenting numerous Latin synonyms immediately following the English term to be defined. He does not distinguish among the synonyms listed; this he will leave to his students who, though Huloet does not say so, may thus gain a copious vocabulary. This method, despite Huloet's claim, was not without its precedents.

Among the numerous authorities listed at the beginning of his *Abce-*

---

[3] Brandon, *Robert Estienne,* p. 122.

darium is that of Robert Stephanus (Estienne). Estienne published, in 1549, the second edition of his *Dictionnaire françois-latin*. The *Abcedarium* is quite similar to this text in the arrangement and presentation of materials. In listing the term *Cruel,* for example, Estienne places after this word thirteen Latin synonyms. After the same entry, in English, Huloet lists an even larger number of Latin synonyms. In each case the lexicographer follows the main entry *Cruel* with a number of phrases in which the word *cruel* is used—in French by Estienne, in English by Huloet—with Latin equivalents. Although there is some overlapping in the synonyms introduced by the two, there is not enough to warrant a conclusion of direct borrowing by Huloet.

Huloet's debt to his predecessor is rarely for particular words and phrases but to the Estienne text as a model for the arrangement of entries on the page, for the introduction of a larger number of Latin synonyms, and for the suggestion that the uses of the main term be illustrated.

In 1572 John Higgins published a revised and greatly augmented edition of the *Abcedarium* under the title of *Huloet's Dictionarie,* in which he added the French equivalents of the English and Latin definitions. In his address to the reader Higgins acknowledged his debt to Jehan Thierry for the French additions. In 1564 Thierry had revised Robert Estienne's *Dictionnaire françois-latin,* and from this edition Higgins drew the French terms for his expansion of Huloet. Higgins stated that he had placed the letter *S* after all such borrowings to indicate Robert Stephanus as the original author thereof. Though Higgins does not in fact so scrupulously designate every borrowing, the evidence shows heavy indebtedness to the Estienne-Thierry dictionaries.

A few examples which show the relationshp of Higgins to his French predecessors may be seen in the English entries *Assemble, Hide, Combate, Comely, Compte* and their French equivalents *Assēbler, Cacher, Combattre, Convenablement, Compter.* The study of these examples in their respective texts shows that for his vernacular entries Higgins borrowed the Latin synonyms and their French equivalents from Thierry's revised edition of Estienne's *Dictionnaire.*

Estienne's Dictionaries and Baret's *Alvearie*

Of all the dictionaries compiled by English lexicographers in the sixteenth century, John Baret's *An Aluearie, or Triple Dictionarie, in Englishe, Latin and French* (1573) exhibits the most pervasive influence of the French language. This influence comes, directly and indirectly, from the dictionaries of Robert Estienne. The method used by Baret and his collaborators in putting together the materials of the *Alvearie* makes it difficult to determine exactly how and when the French influence on the *Alvearie* was exerted, but Baret's address "To the Reader" sheds light on this problem. The matter pertinent to this discussion may be summarily interpreted. About 1555, eighteen years before the publication of the *Alvearie* (1573), Baret says, he and his pupils at Cambridge began collecting materials for an English-Latin glossary, or vocabulary, to expedite the progress of pupils in the study of Latin. For their purpose they found most helpful a recent edition of the *Bibliotheca Eliotae: Eliotis Librarie* (1552). "Within a yeare or two" (this time may well have been much longer), the students had collected a considerable volume of material (manuscript, of course) derived from rearranging into English-Latin the definitions and illustrations from the *Bibliotheca Eliotae* and from classical authors, such as Cicero, Caesar, Terence, etc.

In the course of a few years the English-Latin glossary thus compiled and already termed an "Alvearie" (but not yet published) was borrowed by "diuers of our friendes" who urged that the manuscript be printed for the "publike propagation of the Latin tongue." This request was resisted "until at length" (probably a few years later), persuaded by "Maister Garth" and "Maister Powle" and others, Baret and his new-found assistants set about revising the text of the manuscript and preparing it for the press. At the same time, i.e., about 1570 to 1572, Baret learned that *Huloet's Dictionarie,* with French terms added to the English and Latin, was soon to be printed. At this time Baret decided to add French to his English-Latin "Alvearie" and also to revise and expand the English and Latin entries to meet what promised to be strong competition. With the help of Robert Estienne's *Dictionarium Latino-Gallicum* for the French, and Cooper's *Thesaurus* for the English and Latin, Baret and his assistants soon overhauled their manuscript and had it ready for publication only a few months after John Higgins, the competing editor, had published his edition of *Huloet's Dictionarie* (1572).[4] If my interpretation of Baret's "Address" seems oversimplified, I admit that it is so, but a close study of Baret's antecedents and contemporaries and a comparison of the various texts involved will, I think, support my conclusion.

The suggestion above that Estienne's *Dictionarium Latino-Gallicum* (1552, 1561) was one of the principal sources of the French in the *Alvearie* does not exclude the revisers' use of additional sources. Much borrowed matter is indeed from an immediate predecessor and competitor, Higgins' edition of *Huloet's Dictionarie* (1572). Although Baret had rejected vehemently the printer's request for permission to use Baret's notes to augment the Huloet work, either he or his collaborators had no scruples in borrowing from this rival volume, published less than a year before the *Alvearie*. As the Higgins edition of Huloet owed much to the Elyot-Cooper dictionaries, and also to Thierry's revised edition of Estienne's *Dictionnaire françois-latin* (1564), it is not easy to determine Baret's debt to Huloet-Higgins. After the possibility of common sources has been taken into consideration, definite evidence remains that even the first edition of the *Alvearie* (1573) owes something to *Huloet's Dictionarie* of 1572. These entries, for example, in Huloet's *Abcedarium*, *Huloet's Dictionarie* edited by Higgins, and the *Alvearie* may be compared: *Gilthed, Activitie, Gymmow, Cupbord*. In each instance Baret's definition follows the phrasing and details of the Huloet-Higgins rather than the earlier Huloet. These entries are representative. In the 1580 edition of the *Alvearie*, Abraham Fleming, the editor, has included more generous borrowings from the Huloet-Higgins, and indirectly further increased the debt to the dictionaries of Estienne.

Very early in this chapter we noted the free borrowing, first of Elyot and then of Cooper, from Estienne's *Dictionarium Latino-Gallicum*. Up to the time Baret decided to revise his manuscript he had depended much for his English-Latin entries upon the Elyot-Cooper *Bibliotheca*. In the process of revision and augmentation, obviously later than 1565, he resorted to Cooper's *Thesaurus*, to correct and augment the English-

4 Starnes, *Renaissance Dictionaries*, pp. 184 ff.

Latin of the *Alvearie,* with the result that hundreds of the earlier definitions from the *Bibliotheca Eliotae* were changed to correspond to the entries in Cooper's *Thesaurus.* Certain word tests seem to show what happened in the revision. Among these words are *Plango, Redimiculum, Remordeo, Supplico, Scopae,* all of which indicate that the final form of the English-Latin definitions and illustrations in the 1573 *Alvearie* was determined by the entries in Cooper's *Thesaurus.* Other comparisons give similar results—for example, the entries in the *Alvearie* from "*C,* 501" to "*C,* 535." In these thirty-five successive entries, except for four which derive from some source other than the Elyot-Cooper dictionaries, the Cooper *Thesaurus* determines the English phrasing. The French influence in all these entries is indirect because it is concealed in the definitions and phrases borrowed much earlier from Estienne and converted into English. But direct indebtedness of the *Alvearie* to Estienne's *Dictionnaire françois-latin* (1549) may be seen in seventy-odd etymologies, as exemplified in such words as *Adventure, Alarme, Almanach, Approche,* and *Attayne.* Also, certain entries not involving etymologies derive from the *Dictionnaire,* such as *To agree to one, Abundance or plenty, Very old or aged.* These are among the entries in the *Alvearie* not explainable by a source such as Estienne's *Dictionarium Latino-Gallicum* or Cooper's *Thesaurus.*

From Jean Veron's edition of Estienne's *Dictionariolum puerorum* (1552), the Baret collaborators gathered some materials, as in these English entries: *Measure—A measure of liquids contayning sixe sextarii; Cast—To cast togither; Winke—To winke with the eyen.*

Of all the Estienne lexicons, the *Dictionarium Latino-Gallicum* (1552, 1561) contributed most to the French terms and, indirectly, to the English in the *Alvearie.* It will be remembered that in the augmentation of the *Bibliotheca,* first Elyot and then Cooper drew freely from an early edition of the *Dictionarium Latino-Gallicum* (1538), and that when Cooper compiled his *Thesaurus,* this Estienne *Dictionarium* was a major source. Thus the English and Latin of the Elyot-Cooper dictionaries had a strong Gallic flavor, which carried over to the *Alvearie.*

Furthermore, Baret and the revisers of the manuscript of the *Alvearie* shortly before its 1573 publication, made the *Dictionarium Latino-Gallicum* a major source for the French entries. By tracing certain key words through the principal English, Latin, and French sources of the *Alvearie* and comparing these with the corresponding entry in Baret's book we may make valid inferences as to what happened in the course of compilation and revision of Baret's *Alvearie*. Note, for example, the definitions of *to abolishe* (*aboleo, abolere*).

Dictionnaire françois-latin
(Estienne—1549)
Abolir, Abolere, Abrogare, Antiquare, Conuellere, Exterminare, Inducere, Interuertere, Obliterare, Resignare, Delere.

Dictionarium Latino-Gallicum
(Estienne—1552, 1561)
Aboleo, aboles, pen. cor. aboleui & abolui, abolitum, pen. cor. abolere. Cic. *Abolir, Mettre a neant, Anichiler.*

Bibliotheca Eliotae
(Elyot-Cooper—1559)
Aboleo, aboles, eui, ere, act. to put out, to rase out, disanull, to undoe foreuer.

Thesaurus linguae Romanae et Britannicae
(Cooper—1565)
Aboleo, aboles, pen. corr. aboleui, & abolui, abolitum, pen. corr. Cic. To abolishe: to undoe: to put out, to rase: to disanull.

An Aluearie, or Triple Dictionarie, in Englishe, Latin, and French
(Baret—1573)
to Abolishe: to vndoe: to repeale: reuerse or disanull: to put out. *Aboles, boles. penult. cor. aboleui & abolui, abolitum, lere.* Cic. *Abrogare, Antiquare, Conuellere, Exterminare, Iuducere, Obliterare, Resignare, Delere. Abolir, Mettre a neant, Anichiler.* [A, 45]

Analysis of the transcribed entries above shows that the *Alvearie* as printed in 1573 owes something to Estienne's *Dictionnaire* and *Dictionarium,* and Cooper's *Thesaurus*. In all probability the earlier manuscript of the *Alvearie* had an entry that corresponded in its English to the *Bibliotheca* (1559), and in its French and Latin to the *Dictionnaire* (1549). The form finally printed may have been the result of revision of the entry on the basis of the *Dictionarium Latino-Gallicum* and the Cooper *Thesaurus*.

The entry *Atrocitie* (and many other words) traced through the various dictionaries mentioned above will show similar results. On the other hand, many entries in the 1573 *Alvearie* show simply a joint use of Estienne's *Dictionarium* and Cooper's *Thesaurus*. Among these entries are: *a Bellowes, a Bragget, Crooked, A craftie beguiler.* Whether this conjectural reconstruction of the way the *Alvearie* was compiled is acceptable or not, the French influence of Estienne's various dictionaries is demonstrable throughout.

Concerning the 1580 edition of the *Alvearie* edited by Abraham Fleming, little need be said. Fleming made many small changes and corrections and added an appendix of 264 Latin-English proverbs, with an index. He retained, however, the entries of the earlier edition of the *Alvearie* showing French influence. In short, we may say that Baret's *Alvearie* shows a more pervasive influence of Estienne's lexicography than does any other bilingual dictionary compiled by an English author in the sixteenth century.

Estienne's Proper-Name Dictionaries and English Authors

Our survey thus far shows how far-reaching was the influence of the Estienne dictionaries on the content and organization of the bilingual and trilingual general dictionaries, exclusive of proper names, in sixteenth-century England. But the survey would not be complete without noting the impact of the Estienne proper-name dictionaries on English lexicographers.

From Cooper's *Thesaurus* (1565) to the beginning of the eighteenth century, the comprehensive Latin-English dictionaries each had a special section devoted to Biblical and classical proper names. The English lexicographers imitated the title of the Estienne *Dictionarium historicum* and translated many of its biographical, legendary, and mythical entries.

A chronological listing of titles of the Estienne proper-name Latin dictionary of 1553 (*Dictionarium historicum*) and subtitles of the Latin-English dictionaries from Cooper to Adam Littleton suggests the persistence of the type:

Date	*Author*	*Title*
1553	Robert Estienne	*Dictionarium historicum ac Poeticum . . .*
1565	Thomas Cooper	Accessit *Dictionarium Historicum & poeticum propria vocabula . . .*

1589	Thomas Thomas	Huic etiam accessit *Dictionarium Historicum &* *Poeticum*
1606–1648	Francis Holyoke	*Index Propriorum, siue Dictionariolum Poeticum* *& Historicum.* "Collected out of Stephanus [Estienne], Gesner and others"
1664	Francis Gouldman	*Dictionarium Historico-Geographico-Poeticum*
1678	Adam Littleton	*Dictionarium Poeticum, Historicum & Geographicum . . .*

"To the English Reader," Littleton writes, "In the Latine Proper [proper names] we have so handled History, Poetick Fiction, and Geography as to confine them, what we might, though overborne with Precedents, even drawn from Stephanus [Estienne] himself (*out of whom the rest have taken most of theirs*) [italics mine] . . . as to give some instance of useful or delightful knowledge." Littleton may have been thinking of the Estienne *Dictionarium historicum,* though he could hardly have been unaware of the Bible glossary, as shown by the details and order of arrangement under such entries as *Abarim, Abdon, Abiah, Abimilech,* and *Abishag.* These reveal his knowledge of Estienne's *Hebraea . . . nomina.*

Poeticus or *poeticum,* as used in the title of proper-name dictionaries from Torrentinus in the fifteenth century to Adam Littleton in the seventeenth, had reference especially to the classical allusions in ancient Greek and Latin literatures. A "Dictionarium poeticum" would, therefore, explain the meanings of the allusions and thereby give its readers a better conception of classical myth and legend. Herein lay its importance. This aim is expressed or implicit in all the title pages and headings of proper-name dictionaries. The Estiennes gave it emphasis and supplemented it with hundreds of examples. The impact of their work on the sixteenth- and seventeenth-century lexicographers in England, and directly or indirectly on English poets and dramatists is, in my opinion, demonstrable beyond a reasonable doubt. Illustrations which follow will support this conclusion.

Cooper's *Dictionarium historicum & poeticum,* appended to his *Thesaurus* (1565), was patterned after the Estienne *Dictionarium historicum ac poeticum* (1553) and was much indebted to it. The result was that when authors borrowed directly from Cooper, their ultimate debt often was to Estienne, as we shall see below. Although the poetic dictionary was intended primarily to benefit the reader of classical literature, it proved to be a boon to the author in the sixteenth century.

Certain allusions to classical mythology in Spenser's poems come from the Estienne *Dictionarium historicum* by way of Cooper. The gloss on the *Graces* in "April" (*Shepheardes Calender* 109), ascribed to the mythical "E. K.," is almost a verbatim transcription of Cooper's descriptive account of the Graces under the entry *Charites*, and Cooper's item is a free translation from the Estienne *Dictionarium historicum*. In the *Faerie Queene* (6. 10. 9 ff.) Spenser treats more elaborately the subject of the Graces. Analysis of the stanzas on the topic in the *Faerie Queene* indicates that the poet was familiar with both the English version of *Charites* in Cooper and the original Latin of Estienne.[5]

In his allusions to the "Hylas myth" (*F.Q.* 3. 12. 7 and 4. 10. 27), Spenser appears to confuse Hylas, the beloved companion of Hercules, with Hyllus, Hercules' son. The details of Spenser's reference as well as his confusion of names may be accounted for by his following the story as related in Cooper, and the English version derives in large part from Estienne. The story of the poet Stesichorus, who was temporarily blinded for writing against Helen but who had his sight restored when he recanted, is used by Spenser in E. K.'s comment in "April" (1. 26), and in *Colin Clouts Come Home Again*. The sketch of Stesichorus in Estienne's *Dictionarium historicum* is the most probable source for this information. Many other allusions in Spenser may also be illuminated by reference to his sources in the Cooper and Estienne dictionaries.

Perhaps the majority of the classical allusions in Shakepeare's poems and plays came to him secondhand. One dictionary with which he was familiar was Cooper's poetic dictionary, included in his *Thesaurus*.[6] In 2 *Henry IV* (2. 2. 94, 98) the Page's mistaken reference to "Althea [who] dreamed she was delivered of a fire brand" has closely corresponding phrasing, *s.v. Hecuba,* in Cooper. Several references to Hercules in the plays (*Love's Labour's Lost* 4. 3. 340–341; *Pericles* 1. 1. 27–29; *Coriolanus* 4. 6. 99–100) indicate mistakes of the playwright because of his dependence on Cooper's description of Hercules' labors. Shakespeare, for example, refers to Hesperides as a "fair gar-

---

[5] The Spenser illustrations are selected, revised, and condensed from Starnes and Talbert's *Classical Myth and Legend in Renaissance Dictionaries,* pp. 50 ff.
[6] *Ibid.,* pp. 112 ff.

den" and to Hercules as climbing the tree and shaking down the fruit. In *The Taming of the Shrew* (1. 2. 71–72) Petruchio asserts that he will marry any woman for wealth, be she

> As old as Sibyl, and as curst and shrewd
> *As Socrates Xanthippe* . . .

Petruchio was probably remembering Cooper on Xanthippe: "A passing shrewde, curst, and a waywarde woman, wife to the pacient and wise philosopher Socrates."

In *Lucrece* the poet uses, among other source materials, two entries—*Tarquinius* and *Lucretia*—from the proper-names section of Cooper's *Thesaurus*:

[Lucius] Tarquinius. For his proud and sterne behaviour surnamed Superbus . . .

is the basis for part of the Argument:

Lucius Tarquinius, for his excessive pride surnamed Superbus . . .

At the end of the item on *Tarquinius,* we read "vide *Lucretia.*" Cooper's concise, informed summary of the Lucrece story is reflected, in incident and phraseology, in the text of Shakespeare's *Lucrece*. Cooper found the source of the sketches of Tarquin and Lucrece in Estienne's *Dictionarium historicum*. He translated the Latin freely, making interpolations from other sources.

As a scholar grounded in Latin and Greek, Ben Jonson could read the classics in the original and, judging from the annotations of the books in his library, often did so. It is, however, now known that he frequently consulted reference books as a matter of economy. We know that he made use of Robert Estienne's *Dictionarium . . . Thesaurus*. He also consulted the Estienne *Dictionarium historicum*.

Professor Talbert demonstrates at length Jonson's use of the Estienne dictionaries. Talbert points out that in the glosses to the *Masque of Queens,* Jonson's sketches of Penthesilea, Camilla, Candace, and Artemisia are based on the Estienne *Dictionarium historicum*. The gloss on Artemisia is of special interest because Jonson, following the dictionaries, confuses the two Artemisias. Again, glosses on the *Masque of Augurs* incorporate mistakes of the dictionaries in the accounts of

Linus and Phoenomoe.[7] Copying the errors of the Estienne lexicons is convincing proof of Jonson's sources, and abundant evidence indicates Jonson's use of these reference books, both in his glosses and in the titles of his masques and plays. It is time, however, to turn to other English writers who are known to have made use of the Estienne proper-name dictionaries.

Thomas Heywood, like Ben Jonson, borrowed from the dictionaries for his glosses, or annotations, as in *Earth and Age* and *Aegeus,* and also for suggestions for developing and illustrating ideas in the text proper of his poems. Though Heywood used other source material, he depended much on the list in Cooper's *Thesaurus* and on the poetic dictionary of Robert Estienne. He used these in the annotations of his classical allusions, as ready references to the original classical sources, and as direct sources for allusions in the text of his writings.[8]

Of John Milton's knowledge of the Estienne dictionaries and his use of them as reference works, I have written at length elsewhere.[9] Among the proper names which suggest the relationship of his poetry to the lexicons are these: *Adonis, Bellerophon, Cassiopeia, Choaspes, Cottyto, Echo, Joshua, Oreb, Proserpina, Siloa, Xerxes.* Four of these, with abbreviated treatment, will serve as typical examples. I have italicized comparable words and phrases.

Choaspes

There Susa by Choaspes, amber stream,
The drink of none but kings.
(*Paradise Regained* 3. 288–289)

No commentary cited by scholars seems better to account for the details in these lines than the following from the Estienne *Dictionarium historicum*:

Choaspis, Medorum fluuius, ad fines Persidis in Tigrum defluens: *cuius aquae tam sunt suaues, vt finitimi reges non alia aqua ad potum vtantur.* Tibullus lib. 4.
Nec qua vel Nilus regia lympha Choaspis profluit.

---

[7] *Ibid.,* pp. 140 ff., 146–147.
[8] *Ibid.,* pp. 213 ff.
[9] *Ibid.,* Chapter VIII, pp. 226 ff.; cf. also Starnes, "A Sixteenth-Century Gloss of the Bible," *Names,* VII (June, 1959).

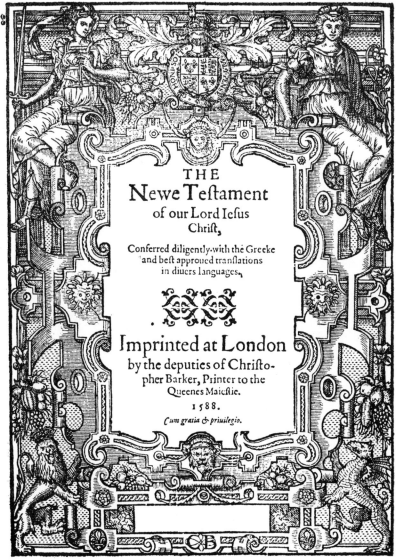

Elizabeth Milton 1654

THE
Newe Teſtament
of our Lord Ieſus
Chriſt,

Conferred diligently with the Greeke
and beſt approued tranſlations
in diuers languages,

Imprinted at London
by the deputies of Chriſto-
pher Barker, Printer to the
Queenes Maieſtie.
1588.

Cum gratia & priuilegio.

FIG. 12. Title page from the New Testament of the Geneva Bible (1588) with the signature of Elizabeth Milton, the poet's third wife.

Compare "the drink of none but kings" and "reges non alia aqua ad potum vtantur."

Echo

Sweet *Echo*, sweetest *Nymph, that liv'st unseen*
Within thy airy shell . . .
Tell me but where,
Sweet Queen of Parley, *Daughter of the Sphere?*
So mayst thou be *translated to the skies,*
And give resounding grace to all *Heaven's Harmonie.*
(*Comus* 11. 230–243)

The conventional myth of Echo and Narcissus never refers to Echo as "daughter of the sphere" or associates her with heavenly harmony. Once again the Estienne poetic dictionary offers this pertinent comment:

Echo, Nympha, nullo oculo visa, et a Pane, pastorum deo, mirum in modum adamata: quae quidem physice *coeli harmoniam significare* dicitur. Solis amicam, tamquam domini et moderatoris *omnium corporum coelestium, ex quibus ipsa componitur atque temperatur.*

In Milton's song, as in Estienne's dictionary, Echo is the Nymph that lives unseen and she is the daughter of the sphere that gives "resounding grace to all Heaven's Harmonies."

Joshua

But *Joshua whom the Gentiles Jesus call,*
His Name and Office bearing, who shall quell
The adversary Serpent . . .
(*Paradise Lost* 12. 310–312)

A part of Milton's lines seems almost a paraphrase of the following entry in Estienne:

Iosue, & Iesus, idem est nomen: cognominatus est autem a patre, Iesus Naue, vel Iosue Bennum, i. filius Naue, vel Nun, quod idem est . . . Comest. in praefa. libri. *Iosue, Typum Iesu. Christi non solum in gestis, verum etiam in nomine gerens,* transit Iordanem.

The parallelism in the italicized passages in the English and Latin is obvious and, at least, a striking coincidence.

As a final illustration, we may consider two words which Milton employs in close association in the passages indicated below:

Siloa (Sion)
... Or if *Sion Hill*
Delight thee more, and *Siloa's Brook that flowed*
Fast by the Oracle of God ...
(*Paradise Lost* 12. 310–312)

Thee *Sion* and the flowr'y *Brooks* beneath
That *wash thy hallow'd feet, and warbling flow* ...
(*Paradise Lost* 3. 30–31)

Estienne's *Hebraea . . . nomina* and, with slight alteration, his *Dictionarium historicum* have these suggestive entries:

Siloe ... Fons est ad radices montis Sion, qui *non perpetuis aquis, sed certis horis diebusque ebullit,* & per terrae concaua & antra saxi durissimi cum mago sonitu uenit ... Est & *piscina* in Ierusalem.

(*Hebraea ... nomina*)

Sion, Aceruus, aut tumulus, vel specula, aut siccitas. *Mons Ierosolymae* (qui alias *Mons domini,* item & *Mons sanctus* dicitur) in cuius vertice erat arx constructa, quae a Davide, ciuitas Dauidis est vocata.

(*Dictionarium historicum*)

In the lines from *Paradise Lost* Milton is writing, metaphorically, of the heavenly Muse Urania and, associating Siloa and Sion with his thought, he remembers also the physical description of Mount Sion and Siloa brook as presented in Estienne.

Robert Estienne was a Christian humanist. Like Erasmus and other spiritual antecedents, he sought to make classic culture and the will of God prevail in his own day. His high hopes seemed to him within the scope of realization because of his knowledge of printing and his heritage of a fine printing establishment. His efforts to achieve his aims took two directions, parallel and sometimes overlapping: (1) careful editing and printing of the ancient languages and literatures and the supplying of aids for the study of these in the way of glossaries and dictionaries—Latin, Greek, and Hebrew; (2) repeated editing and printing of the Bible, in whole or part, together with glossaries and indexes.

My aim in this study has been to sketch briefly the background of Estienne's career and to trace, in some detail, the persistence and influence of his lexical labors on subsequent lexicographers and authors. The *Hebraea . . . nomina,* prepared for the earlier editions of the *Biblia* and printed independently in 1537, was a treasure-trove for editors of the several polyglot Bibles and the Geneva Bible Concordance and, before the end of the sixteenth century, was incorporated into Estienne's proper-name *Dictionarium historicum,* where it had a secondary existence for at least another century.

The *Dictionarium historicum ac poeticum,* here identified as essentially the work of Robert Estienne, became one of the most popular reference books of the Renaissance. Its vogue on the Continent and in England was very wide; I have tried in this chapter to suggest its impact on English lexicographers and on English poets and dramatists. In a similar way I have dealt with the *Dictionarium . . . Thesaurus,* the *Dictionarium Latino-Gallicum,* and the smaller dictionaries of Estienne. Extensive though their influence was on the Continent, my effort here has been to trace their impact in England.

BIBLIOGRAPHY

Ainsworth, Robert. *Thesaurus linguae Latinae compendiarius: or, A Compendious Dictionary of the Latin Tongue . . . In Three Parts.* London: Printed for J. P. Knapton, M DCC XXXVI.

Armstrong, Elizabeth. *Robert Estienne: Royal Printer.* Cambridge, 1954.

Baret, John. *An Aluearie or Triple Dictionarie, in Englishe, Latin and French.* Folio. London: H. Denham, 1573.

———. *An Aluearie or Quadruple Dictionarie,* Containing Foure Sundrie Tongues [English, Latin, Greek, French]. London: H. Denham, 1580.

Brandon, Edgar Ewing. *Robert Estienne et le dictionnaire français, Au XVIe Siècle.* Baltimore, 1904.

Brunet, Jacques Charles. *Manuel du Libraire et de l'Amateur de livres.* 5 vols. Bruxelles, 1838.

Burckhardt, Jacob. *The Civilization of the Renaissance in Italy.* Translated by S. G. C. Middlemore. Vienna and New York, n.d.

Clark, Evert Mordecai. "Early Geneva Bibles in The University of Texas Library," *Texas Quarterly,* II (Winter, 1959), 167–185.

Cooper, Thomas. *Thesaurus Linguae Romanae & Britannicae.* Impressum Londini, 1565. (Other editions: 1573, 1578, 1584, 1587.)

Cruden, Alexander. *A Complete Concordance of the Holy Scriptures of the Old and New Testament: In Two Parts.* London: Printed for D. Midwinter, D. Bettesworth, M DCC XXXVIII. (Other editions: 1761, 1769, 1785, 1794 . . . 1958.)

———. *Cruden's Concordance to the Old and New Testaments.* A reprint of the second edition. Westwood, New Jersey, 1958.

Darlow, T. H. and H. F. Moule. *Historical Catalogue of the Printed Editions of Holy Scripture in the Library of the British and Foreign Bible Society.* 2 vols. London, 1903.

DeJordy, Alma, and Harris F. Fletcher (eds.). *A Library for Younger Scholars. (Studies in Language and Literature.)* Urbana, Illinois, 1960.

Dore, J. R. *Old Bibles, or An Account of the Various Versions of the English Bible.* London, 1876. (Second edition, augmented, 1888.)

Elyot, Sir Thomas. *The Dictionary of Syr Thomas Elyot, knyght.* Londini in aedibus Thomae Berteleti impress, 1538.

———. *Bibliotheca Eliotae: Eliotis Librarie,* London, 1542, 1545. (Other editions of *Bibliotheca,* augmented by Thomas Cooper: 1548, 1552, 1559.)

Estienne, Robert. *Biblia.* Parisiis: Ex officina Roberti Stephani, 1527–1528. (Other editions: 1532, 1534, 1540, 1546.)

————. *Dictionarium, seu linguae Latinae Thesaurus.* Parisiis: Ex officina Roberti Stephani, M. D. XXXI. (Other editions: 1536, 2 vols.; 1543, 3 vols.; 1573, 4 vols.; 1740, 4 vols., folio.)

————. *Hebraea, Chaldaea, Graeca et Latina nomina.* Parisiis: Ex officina Roberti Stephani, M. D. XXXVII.

————. *Elucidarius poeticus, siue dictionarium nominum propriorum virorum.* Antuerpiae: Ex officina Ioannis Loëi, Anno M. CCCCC. XLV.

————. *Dictionarium Latino-Gallicum.* Lutetiae: Apud Carolum Stephanum, typographum Regium, 1561 (a reprint of 1552 edition).

————. *Dictionarium historicum ac poeticum.* Lutetiae: Cura ac diligentia Caroli Stephani. M. D. LIII.

Ferguson, W. K. *The Renaissance in Historical Thought.* New York, 1948.

Gouldman, Francis. *A Copious Dictionary in Three Parts.* London: Printed by John Field, M. DC. LXIV. (Other editions: 1669, 1674, 1678.)

Greswell, William Parr. *A View of the Early Parisian Greek Press; Including the Lives of the Stephani.* 2 vols. Oxford, 1833.

Harnik, Henry. "Three Interpretations of the French Renaissance," *Studies in the Renaissance,* New York, 1960.

Helvicus, Christopher. *The Historical and Chronological Theatre of Christopher Helvicus . . .* Faithfully done into English. London: Printed by M. Fletcher, M DCL XXXVIII.

Holyoke, Francis. *Riders Dictionarie Corrected and Augmented.* Wherein Riders Index is transformed into a Dictionarie Etymologicall . . . With a brief Index of proper names. Collected out of Stephanus (Estienne), Gesner, and others. London: Printed by Adam Islip, 1606. (Seven other editions appeared at intervals from 1612 to 1659.)

Holyoke, Thomas. *A Large Dictionary in Three Parts.* London, 1677.

Huloet, Richard. *Abcedarium Anglico Latinum, pro Tyrunculis.* Londini: Ex officina Gulielmi Riddell, Anno M. D. LII.

————. *Huloets Dictionarie, Newly corrected by J. Higgins.* London, 1572.

Lee, Sir Sidney. *The French Renaissance in England;* An Account of the Literary Relations of England and France in the Sixteenth Century. Oxford, 1910.

Littleton, Adam. *A Latin Dictionary, in Four Parts.* London, 1678. (Other editions: 1684, 1693, 1703, 1713, etc.)

McMurtrie, Douglas C. *The Book: The Story of Printing and Bookmaking.* Third edition revised. New York and London, 1953.

Marbeck, John. *A Concordance,* That Is To Saie, a Worke wherein Ye May Finde Any Worde in the Whole Bible. London, 1550. (The first English concordance of the whole Bible.)

Michelet, Jules. *La Renaissance,* Vol. VII of *Histoire de France (Ouevres Complètes,* 40 vols.) Paris, 1855.

Minsheu, John. *Ductor in Linguas, The Guide into Tongues.* In Undecim Linguis. London, 1617, 1627.

————. *Minshaei emendatio.* London, 1625, 1626, 1627.

Oliver, Peter. *The Scripture Lexicon, or Dictionary of above Three Thousand Proper Names of Persons and Places mentioned in the Bible.* Birmingham, England: Printed by Piercy and Jones, M, DCC, LXXXIV. (Other editions: 1787, 1792, 1797, 1810, 1818.)

———. *Peter Oliver's Origin and Progress of the American Rebellion: A Tory View.* Edited by Douglass Adair and John Schutz. San Marino, California, 1961.

Panofsky, Erwin. "The Renaissance and Renascences," *The Kenyon Review,* VI (1944), 201–236.

Pocock, Nicholas. "The Bible in the British Museum," *The Quarterly Review.* 178 (London, 1894), 157 ff.

Pollard, Alfred W. *Records of the English Bible: The Documents Relating to the Translation and Publication of the Bible in English, 1525–1611.* London and New York, 1911.

Prince, Thomas. *A Chronological History of New England: In the Form of Annals* [1602–1730]. Boston, 1736.

Renouard, Antoine Augustin. *Annales de l'Imprimerie des Estienne, ou, Histoire de la Famille des Estienne et de ses Éditions.* Deuxième edition. 2 vols. (Burt Franklin Bibliographical and Reference Series No. 20.) New York, 1960.

Rider, John. *Bibliotheca Scholastica, A Double Dictionarie.* Oxford: Printed by Joseph Barnes, Printer to the Vniversitie of Oxford, 1589.

———. *Riders Dictionarie.* Revised by Francis Holyoke (see Holyoke, Francis).

Rollins, Hyder E., and Herschel Baker. *English Renaissance.* Boston, 1954.

Sandys, John Edwin. *A History of Classical Scholarship, from the Revival of Learning to the End of the Eighteenth Century.* 3 vols Cambridge, 1908.

Schaff, Philip (ed.). *A Religious Encyclopedia: or Dictionary of Biblical, Doctrinal, and Practical Theology.* Revised edition. 3 vols. Chicago, New York, London, 1887.

———, and Johann Herzog. *The New Schaff-Herzog Encyclopedia of Religious Knowledge.* Edited by Samuel M. Jackson. 12 vols. New York and London, 1909.

Seebohm, Frederic. *The Oxford Reformers: John Colet, Erasmus, and Thomas More.* Being a history of their fellow-work. London and New York, 1913.

Sibley's Harvard Graduates. Edited by Clifford K. Shipton. 11 vols., 1873–1960. Boston, Massachusetts. VIII, 737–762.

Starnes, D. T. "The Poetic Dictionary and the Poet," *The Library Chronicle,* II (1946), 75–85.

———. *Renaissance Dictionaries: English-Latin and Latin-English.* Austin, Texas, 1954.

———. "A Sixteenth-Century Gloss of the Bible," *Names,* VII (June, 1959), 101–106.

———, and Ernest W. Talbert. *Classical Myth and Legend in Renaissance Dictionaries.* Chapel Hill, North Carolina, 1956.

Thomas, Thomas. *Dictionarium Linguae Latinae et Anglicanae.* Cantabrigae: Ex officina Thomae Thomasii, inclytae Academicae Typographi [1587]. (Fourteen editions from 1587 to 1644.)

Veron, Jean. *Dictionariolum puerorum, tribus linguis, Latina, Anglica, et Gallica conscriptum.* London, 1552.

———. *A Dictionary in Latin and English,* Corrected by R. Waddington. London, 1575.

Wilson, Thomas. *A Christian Dictionarie.* London, 1612. (Other editions, augmented: 1616, 1622, 1630(?).)

Withals, John. *A Shorte Dictionarie Englishe and Latin for Yonge Beginners.* London, 1553. (Numerous other editions until the year 1634.)

INDEX